The Healthy Family

Start EATING FORWARD™

Revised and Updated Edition

Sandi Richard

Kelly Brett M.D.
and George Lambros M.D.

Cooking for the Rushed Inc.

Published by Cooking for the Rushed Inc.
www.cookingfortherushed.com

For information about special discounts for bulk purchases go to
www.cookingfortherushed.com

Library and Archives Canada Cataloguing in Publication

Richard, Sandi, 1959-
    The healthy family : start eating forward / Sandi Richard,
Kelly Brett and George Lambros. -- Rev. and updated ed.

(Cooking for the rushed)
Includes indexes.
ISBN 978-0-9685226-4-6

    1. Nutrition. 2. Quick and easy cookery. I. Brett, Kelly, 1962- II. Lambros,
George, 1964- III. Title. IV. Series: Richard, Sandi, 1959- . Cooking for the rushed.

TX833.5.R524 2010   641.5'63   C2010-901503-7

Printed in Canada   Transcontinental Printing

10 9 8 7 6 5 4 3 2 1

To our readers and to our readers with diabetes
The Healthy Family : Start Eating Forward™ is not a cookbook which claims to cater to the complex dietary needs of a
person with diabetes. The nature of this book is speed and nutrition. A large number of North Americans have some form of
diabetes; therefore we feel it is helpful to provide information on food exchanges and food choice values.

In view of the complex nature of health in relation to food and activity, this book is not intended to replace professional or
medical advice. The authors and publisher expressly disclaim any responsibility for any liability, loss, or risk, personal or otherwise, which is incurred as a consequence, directly or indirectly, of the use and application of any of the contents of this book.

Foreword

The number of North Americans classified as obese has increased dramatically in the last decade in spite of public health programs designed to reduce obesity. High fat, high energy food is readily available (including in our schools), is inexpensive to purchase and contributes to the problem. As of today, Amazon.com stocks 26,418 books under "diet" and Google.com lists 4.1 million web-sites for "food books." How do ordinary people like you and I make sense of all the information on such an important topic as nutrition and healthy eating? Sandi, Kelly and George are trying to address this problem, by filtering all this information to provide parents with the key information necessary to help build healthy eating habits.

This book is not just about diet and food. It covers many important topics of concern related to child health. The book is written in a "down home" style that avoids intimidating, complex concepts and terms. It is light-hearted, factual, practical and simple to read. This is the kind of information we need, presented in a format that is appropriate for a very large audience.

We all know that healthy living includes nutrition and if we have a handle on diet, we gain confidence in the fact we are doing right by our children. Our goal should be to expect a healthy life, not just a long one!

As a physician, my goal is to be an advocate for physical activity, nutrition, and health. Most physicians are aware that the "Energy Balance" the authors of this book speak about has not been widely adopted across North America. Sandi, Kelly and George have taken a necessary and unusual approach to dealing with these complex issues: they've simplified them. They've given us a starting point with each area of food science and meal planning. They have accomplished the objective of their mission -- you will find this book easy to read, interesting, and provocative.

Gordon Matheson MD, PhD
Chief, Division of Sports Medicine
Stanford University
Editor-in-Chief,
The Physician and Sportsmedicine

Table of Contents

Table of Contents

MEAL PLANS

Table of Contents

photo by Paige Macpherson

Introduction:
A North American Crisis

Sounds alarming, doesn't it? Well, let's look at the facts.

The average North American family does not make a million dollars, they do not have a cook, they don't have a nanny, they drive their own kids to their extra curricular activities and they don't look like models. Most of the time when we read about food and fitness, we get an elite point of view, which caters to a very small percentage of the population who are already receptive to health changes. We need to start thinking about the majority of the struggling population, and what will help them!

We hear that we can be healthy if we eat like the people of every other place in the world but ours. This is supposed to fix us all! The fact is, we don't live anywhere else. We live here and we have tons of things on our minds and too many things on our plates, and I don't mean food. We don't have the same economic condition as other places whose diets we are supposed to mimic. Do they have television commercials pounding products into their children's brains every two seconds? Do the parents work day and night to keep up with the North American dream? Do they have more processed and takeout food available than any other place in the world? No!!!

"I'm sooo confused!!!" I hear this all the time. Here's an example of the confusion…the ever popular high-protein, low-carb fad diet. First of all, let's get real here…A high percentage of the population are single parents. How many of those are bringing in an income that can barely meet their rent? So here is a single parent, trying to make ends meet, but they're going to run out and buy only the two most expensive things in the supermarket. Meat and produce. Cooooome on!!! Let's give our heads a shake!

**If we are to change the health of families in North America
we must understand all of their struggles!!!**

North Americans have a time crisis as well as a food crisis.

I speak all over the country and it always blows me away that many women are still feeling guilty that they can't do it all; that, in addition to their careers, they can't always drive Johnny to hockey, Katie to dancing, along with their 12,000 friends, only to return home, pluck the feathers from the chicken for tonight's dinner while simultaneously bathing the baby and then voila…sexy beauty queen mommy appears. I don't think so!!!

My parents are the first to admit that the pressures of our generation are different than what they experienced, but our generation can't admit to itself that we're not pulling "it" off very well. We keep looking for quick fix solutions, only to feel more alone and discouraged when we discover the quick fix is neither quick nor a fix.

Let's face it. We're in big trouble when it comes to food, time and activity. It's not getting better, it's getting worse.

Introduction...(cont.)

We have more information at our fingertips about food and fitness than we've ever had. North Americans purchase more diet and fitness books than any other kind, yet the rate of overweight boys rose from 15 per cent in 1981 to 35 per cent in 1996, and in girls from 15 per cent to 30 per cent in the same time period.

North American crisis? How does this happen? We eat haphazardly and we don't move around enough to burn off the calories we've eaten. I think we need to look at this and take some action now, before it's too late to reverse. A large part of the problem is that we don't Eat Forward™, so while our lives are already out-of-control in other areas, we compound our stress by having chaos around dinner. We often find ourselves in the drive-through lane or eating out of a box, or we spontaneously show up at the grocery store and spend more money than we normally would. As a result, activity becomes a neglected priority.

Think about the financial picture, simply put, eating at home saves money! We'll talk about that in the next few pages. I'd like you also to think about relationships in your family and how things might be a little calmer if eating was a family gathering. Studies show that the average parent spends less than 20 minutes talking one-on-one with their children **per week** while the average child from age 2 to 11 watches 2 hours (and growing) of T.V. **per day**.

The Solution

Get dinner off your mind by getting your family involved, creating Eat Sheets™ and turfing old fashioned methods that don't work in today's busy lifestyles.

How the Docs Fit In

This book, I hope, will help us see things as they really are and give us some tools to get our lives back under control. I was so excited to learn that Dr. Kelly Brett and Dr. George Lambros shared the same passion about keeping families healthy. They've been working for years trying to educate people that regular physical activity doesn't have to be complicated. I've been working for years trying to simplify healthy dinners. Their straight forward, get real approach is refreshing. For the first time, even I really understood calories, energy balance, and their relation to food. As the doctors were working with kids and their families, they were seeing what I was seeing: people just too confused about what is right, what is wrong and how fitness and food relate.

Watch what happens!

This is a one-of-a-kind presentation of real facts. Seven weeks of healthy dinners, including printable Eat Sheets™ (grocery lists) from our web site, that are so delicious you will think it's impossible that you're eating healthy. It's packed with information from the doctors, which is unbelievably easy to read and understand! Even your children will be amazed and fascinated. It's about getting the family together by organizing dinner. It's about getting families active. It's about turning a nation around on its ear while we watch it enjoy the results. It's about teaching our children to care about food and activity like we taught them to care about recycling. Let's begin with the children and the family and let's turn this thing around!

Eating Forward™ Is Freedom

I have chosen pizza for **dinner** tonight –my family will be so excited!

...therefore I will have vegetables and protein such as grilled chicken on spinach salad for **lunch**.

...therefore I should have a fruit smoothy or oatmeal with fruit and nuts or whole-wheat toast with light peanut butter for **breakfast**.

Normal food + knowing what you are eating for dinner = Eating Forward™

When you are Eating Forward™ you don't think about dinner all day, you don't hound anyone to help make that decision mid day--you are at peace. You feel great! There is emotional and physical balance! Instinctively you know how to eat during the course of the day, based on what you will eat at dinner. Everything is connected! Your body is in sync with your mind. Your mind is at ease, your sugars are balanced - you emotionally feel great about how you eat and how you feed your family. Your body has no need to store fat, it's happy; it knows you aren't throwing it a curve ball. You are emotionally in tune with dinner. It's a nurturing time for your body and for your family.

Now …What's typical?

North American's typical day

Run out the door for work- nothing is taken out for dinner. Have no idea what you will be eating at dinner. Grab a coffee, and possibly a muffin, for **breakfast** on the way to work. Get the 10:00 A.M. sugar shakes. Eat whatever is convenient which is usually high starch processed food.

Get food from the most convenient source for **lunch**, either local fast food (let's say today you choose pizza), or something you have brought from home.

Eating Forward™ (cont.)

2ish in the afternoon - You likely phone your partner asking what they want for dinner or begin making a decision what dinner is on your own, based on emotions and your evening schedule. If your partner doesn't answer appropriately, you feel frustrated and it may even affect your relationship negatively that evening.

Get home, to the new demands of the day - either make something convenient for **dinner** or maybe your partner ordered in, let's say...pizza, seeing the kids schedule is full that night.

Do you see how dinner is actually an emotional and time problem - creating a food problem?

The North American's typical day leaves you constantly thinking about dinner all day long! Your mind is preoccupied. It feels like you've spent hours on dinner between thinking about it, asking about it, then having to cook it at the end of the day. It feels like it's taken hours out of your day - because it has!

How could you know how to balance your food during the day? It doesn't mean that it wouldn't balance accidently sometimes, it's just less likely because nothing is connected. My nephew, Dane attends university and loves to cook. He challenged me on my theory saying, "Well I could do this exact thing the other way. I could choose my breakfast, then choose my lunch making sure I don't choose the same sorts of foods, then choose my dinner also making sure I balance dinner with what I already ate for breakfast and lunch." I explained, "Well that's fine if you're single and are really doing that! If you have the type of life where at the end of your day you can focus on food and nothing else…it can be done! Most people have a life where schedules are complex and there are other people involved, such as partners and children. It's very unlikely you will be able to block out life while managing to choose what you're eating, evaluating what you ate that day, and then cook dinner!!" My nephew got it!

You have no idea how deep rooted negative feelings can be when the "Asker of the meals" doesn't have a clue what dinner is going to be that night. What does the "Asker of the meals" mean? There is always one in every family situation. One person tends to take on the task of knowing what dinner will be each night. Soooo, because this person is already trying to be thoughtful enough to organize this, they are also thoughtful enough to ask other people in the family what they want to eat for dinner, especially their partner. This turns sour, when the partner answers, "I don't know"! The "Asker of the meals" suddenly feels abandoned and the dinner task, strapped with emotion, feels larger than it actually is!

Eating Forward™ Steps

If you know you are having cheesy lasagna for dinner, will you want to eat that same thing for lunch? Instinctively you will choose something different. When you choose different foods your diet is balanced naturally. No counting, no stressing, no deprivation.

Diets, for the most part, are only sustainable for just a few weeks because diets do not incorporate life's busyness! When a person cannot sustain a diet, they beat themselves up and feel like a failure. By contrast, repeat the following steps for just a few weeks and life actually gets easier! This is because you now have three weeks of reuseable Eat Sheets™ that your family has created. No nagging, no fretting, no guilt. Just easy dinners your family has chosen.

Five Basic Steps to Change Dinner Time Forever

1. Go to www.eatingforward.com and print off a blank Eat Sheet™. Tack it in a central location in the kitchen. Use the Eat Sheets™ in the back of this book as an example of how to set it up. See page 163.

Tell your family members to give you dinner suggestions for meals they will actually eat. You will likely need to ask over and over again. If necessary warn them, if they don't pick, you will. Believe me, it's worth the short term hassle.

2. At the top left of your Eat Sheet™ write down their meal suggestions and which recipe book they can be found in. Make sure the five meals are not all the same. You need a variety of meals to keep your week nutritionally balanced! If two people have chosen something similar ask someone to change their first pick, promising to transfer that meal to the following week.

Eating Forward™ Steps (cont.)

3.   Pour yourself a tea or a glass of red, find the five recipes the family has chosen and transfer every single ingredient from each recipe to the Eat Sheet™. DO NOT LEAVE INGREDIENTS OFF THE LIST EVEN IF YOU HAVE THEM IN THE HOUSE. This is a reuseable Eat Sheet™, NOT THE LIST YOU WILL TAKE TO THE STORE. Write the ingredients under each category according to where you will find those items at your particular grocery store. Don't forget to include ingredients you serve with the main course, if the recipe doesn't include side dishes.

Put your Eat Sheet™ in a plastic sheet protector and put that in a small binder close to your recipe books. Show EVERYONE where it is so that Step 4 can be easily delegated.

4.   Use your Eat Sheet™ to check which groceries you will need to purchase at the grocery store to complete your week of meals. The beauty of the Eat Sheet™ is that it is so complete. Anyone can use it to make a shopping list of the ingredients you will need to purchase for those meals on any given week!

Our readers tell us they create their shopping lists from the Eat Sheet™ in different ways. Some cross off items they don't need to purchase using a washable marker on the plastic sheet protector. Some use a separate piece of paper to jot down the items they need. Some go to www.eatingforward.com and customize their Eat Sheet™, save to their computer, print, then cross off the items they don't need.

5.   Go buy your groceries! Then, every night at dinner discuss with your family which meal fits your schedule for the following night. Take out the stuff you'll need to defrost.

Each week you follow these steps you will add a new Eat Sheet™ to your binder.

On a week you just can't do this, use one that's already done.

Medical Gobbledygook

As doctors, there are advantages and disadvantages when it comes to co-authoring a book focused on the healthy family. One advantage is that we are able to combine our medical knowledge with our passion for the subject. One disadvantage is that we think and talk like doctors! We recognize every profession has its peculiar lingo. Anyone who has tried to understand the computer guy describing how a computer program works knows this all too well. This applies to the mechanic, the accountant or the cook. Without an understanding of the subject matter being discussed, it sounds like gobbledygook. "Hey, would you just talk in English!"

Doctors are renowned for using big words and leaving their patients totally confused. For most of us MDs, this is not an egocentric plot to make ourselves look smarter than our patients; that's just how we talk. It is easier for doctors to use the term coronary artery bypass graft (commonly shortened to "cabbage"), rather than "an operation where the chest wall is opened up, the heart is exposed and pieces of vein are taken from the legs and used to bypass a blockage in the blood vessels supplying the heart". Hey, to us it's just a cabbage! We spend years learning the language of medicine and it just becomes part of our vocabulary. The problem is that most people are more concerned about their health than their computer, so when doctors talk the talk, our patients often leave our office with more questions than answers.

In this book we are trying to present medical information in such a way that it actually makes sense to the average person. This really came to light during one of our editorial meetings when we were trying to explain to Sandi, Ron, Pat, and Tannie why proteins are so important. We were so excited about describing the chemical structure of proteins, how they are synthesized in cells, how the body metabolizes them and so on. How can you not get excited about this great stuff? Apparently by the reaction from the gang, we missed the boat about what was important to most people about protein!

Some people have used confusion about nutrition and exercise to promote wonder diets and revolutionary exercise programs which promise to make us all look like models. People buy into this propaganda because they really hope they can find a quick and easy way to lose flab and have muscles bulging all over the place. It just doesn't work that way and a lot of people don't have the background knowledge to sort out all this hype. If a mechanic told us that using a "special" additive in our gas tank every day would turn our beater car into a Mercedes, we would laugh (although some people would probably still buy it!). We just have to walk into a mega vitamin store to hear the same story, but in this case, we believe it. There is always some miracle supplement which promises to make us healthier and help us live longer. The same is true with diets. We learn that a certain doctor-recommended diet high in protein is the answer to all our problems, but in the same magazine, a diet high in carbohydrates is promoted as better to help us shed those unsightly pounds.

Here *is* something you can hang your hat on. The vast majority of fad diets and mega doses of vitamins and minerals have not proven to be of any long-term benefit and some have actually been found to be dangerous. There is no quick fix for good health.

We hope that our explanations will help people realize that the way to long lasting health is through good eating habits and regular physical activity.

What Gives You Energy Can Also Make You Fat

When I travel across the country, one of the things I'm asked by all kinds of different people is, "What's real and what's hype?" People are so confused about food. One minute we hear it's not good to eat lots of meat…then we read we should be loading up on protein-rich foods like meats and not on carbohydrate-rich food like pastas and grains. The next thing we hear is that we should be loading up on fruits and vegetables…and now people say, be careful which ones you choose as they too are loaded with carbs!!!!! Yiiiikes. I know I felt this way when I was overweight many years ago. I didn't know what to do from one minute to the next. Then I learned that we need food to give us energy. All kinds of different delicious mmmmmoan-worthy food. We need to enjoy the experience while we are eating. Healthy food has to be delicious! We just have to know when to eat, how much to eat and how it relates to our activity. Let's ask the doctors to explain to us how energy and food are connected so that we actually get it. Go for it, Kelly and George.

From the Doctors

Well, energy is simply the ability of something to do work. For us humans, that "work" is as basic as walking *or* as challenging as running the Boston Marathon. Where does this energy come from? Easy, from the food we eat. Food fuels our body, whether it comes from a peanut butter sandwich, a glass of milk, or a piece of chocolate. Energy comes from the breakdown of chemical bonds in the food. Every substance on earth has chemical bonds but our body's "chemistry set" can only use certain types of stuff to produce energy, namely carbohydrates, proteins and fats found in plants and animals.

Scientists use the metric system when they do all their fancy calculations. We generally talk about how much energy is in a gram of food (there are 28 grams in an ounce). Carbohydrates (like sugar and starch) and protein have 4 Calories of energy in a gram, while fat has 9 Calories per gram. Our body uses enzymes to break down these foods to produce energy.

Burning Energy *		
Activity	Calories/min 100 lb person	Calories/min 150 lb person
Basketball	6.2	9.3
Cycling (5 mph)	2.9	4.3
Cycling (9 mph)	4.3	6.5
Dance (high intensity)	7.3	10.9
Football	6.0	9.0
In-line skating (12 mph)	8.7	13.1
Skipping Rope (slow)	6.8	10.2
Skipping Rope (fast)	8.3	12.5
Running (8 min/mile)	8.8	13.2
Running (11 min/mile)	6.0	9.0
Step aerobics (6 inch step)	5.0	7.5
Soccer	6.3	9.4
Swimming (fast crawl)	7.0	10.5
Tennis	4.7	7.1
Strength training (endurance)	5.0	7.5
Walking	3.5	5.2
Mowing the grass	5.0	7.5
Raking the grass	2.5	3.7
Working with a shovel	4.4	6.6
Cleaning the house	2.3	3.4

* The energy expenditure for an activity varies based on a person's weight, gender, age and metabolic rate.

In reality, the body is a very, very complex machine and a very smart one. It can provide energy to your muscles (so you can walk, laugh or blink your eyes), or to your brain so you can think, and to a whole bunch of other places, too.

So lots of energy (fuel) must be great, right? After all, lots of gas would keep your car running forever, but your car's fuel tank can only hold so much gas and then it overflows. The more you use your car and the faster you drive, the more gas you use. Your body works the same way (except it doesn't get rusty…sorry, we couldn't resist!). The more active you are, the more fuel you burn. The trick with eating and drinking is to put the same amount of fuel in as you are burning up. Too little fuel and the car slows down and stops. Too much fuel and the gas spills all over the ground. Instead of spilling the fuel, your body stores the extra energy it can't use as fat. We all need some stored fat to be healthy but too much is not the best thing for us.

"Burn Baby Burn"

Use the information in the tables of "Burning Energy" and "You Decide" to calculate how long you have to do an activity to burn off different foods.

Take the energy found in a food and divide it by the energy for a particular activity (e.g. riding your bike).

One chocolate covered granola bar = 144 Calories

Cycling (medium intensity) for one minute uses 6.5 Cal/minute

144 Cal divided by 6.5 Cal/minute = 22 minutes

1 1/2 hours to burn off 1 up-sized french fries

Biking may not be your thing - but the point is - the guy in front is finished burning off his calories after having a whole satisfying meal. The guy behind still has another half hour to ride and he only ate fries!

1 hour to burn off the Tangy Chicken meal

22 minutes to burn off just one chocolate covered granola bar!!!!!

You Decide

(Based on a 150 lb person cycling at medium intensity)

Energy	Cal.	Activity Minutes
Cookie-chocolate chip	50	7
Doughnut-sour cream glazed	320	49
Water	0	0
Cola type soda 10 oz	133	20
One toasted large pita, brushed with oil, sprinkled with sugar and cinnamon	276	42
Take-out cinnamon bun average size	720	110

Energy	Cal.	Activity Minutes
Whole meal tangy baked chicken (2 thighs, rice and veggie)	436	67
One serving of up-sized fries	569	87
Munching on 1 large stick of celery with low-fat dip	53	8
Munching on 20 potato chips	210	32
Chicken breast marinated and broiled	294	45
Chicken breast fried with batter	728	112

Sandi's Tips

So you see, it's not a problem to have a doughnut or a piece of deep fried chicken from time to time. The problem is when you're eating like this and aren't very active. Your body will store the excess energy as fat. A solution is to increase your activity level and choose healthier food more often.

My Food Beliefs

I believe Eating Forward™ is the only way North Americans will be able to get back to the dinner table. We need to get dinner off our minds! Only then will we be able to balance our eating in the day and actually look forward to the dinner hour!

Nutritious food should be fast and delicious; otherwise you may eat something you shouldn't.

There is a time for frozen and there is a time for fresh. I use well washed fresh veggies at the front of the week and frozen toward the end. This keeps me from going back to the grocery store. For those worried about the nutritional value of frozen, keep in mind food manufacturers are able to remove much of the residual chemicals from the frozen veggies for you, so it's O.K. to let someone else do the work when you're in a rush.

Meats should be trimmed, so purchase them that way. You don't have time to trim. Boneless, skinless chicken is best. Don't tell yourself you can't afford it, tell yourself you need that help to cook quickly. Besides, are you really saving money when buying untrimmed or cheaper cuts? When I buy 1 3/4 pounds of untrimmed steak, I end up with a little over a pound, and worse, trimming takes extra time I don't have!

Carbohydrates are great souces of energy. Dry pasta, rice and potatoes are easy to store and easy to make. Use different varieties of pasta and rice to make meals more interesting. It's okay to buy dehydrated potato flakes, canned potatoes or dehydrated potato slices as a back-up. Using fresh potatoes is best, but without a back-up take-out might end up being the alternative.

If you have kids, remember, **you're not running a restaurant.** You need to provide them with a protein, a carbohydrate and a fruit or vegetable at dinner. Some may be meat eaters and some may be vegetarians. Most will like the carbohydrate. Make a rule that they must have a very small taste of the part they hate. Don't let them snack an hour later if they don't eat the part of dinner they usually like; otherwise you are giving your stamp of approval for poor eating habits.

Buying your groceries in advance saves you money; that's why we provide you with **Eat Sheets™** you can photocopy or download from our website. We also provide you with fill in the blanks **Eat Sheets™**. If you don't like the way our weeks are set up, go ahead and set up your own. One of the most frequent comments we received from test families was, "I don't get it. I'm buying helpers and better quality meats but my grocery bill has gone down." Do you know why? It's because you're not buying extra stuff. I don't know about you, but it costs me 25 bucks every time I go into a store to buy a loaf of bread!!! If your groceries are already in the house for that week's meals, you'll save money, because you don't need to be walking into a store every second day. Think about that!!

✔ Food must be "to die for" delicious

✔ Food must be quick to prepare

✔ Food must be found at a regular grocery store

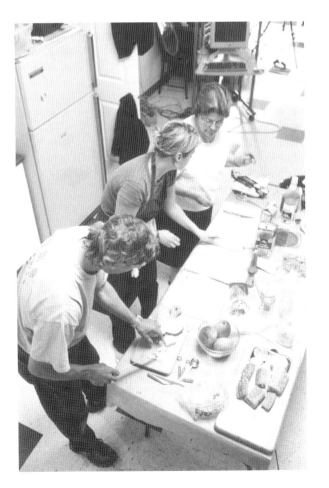

Your Body is Like a Cake…Sort of

From the Doctors

In the upcoming sections we are going to try and explain why a balanced diet of carbohydrates, fats, proteins, vitamins and minerals is important for good health. We are constantly bombarded with information about these nutrients but few people, including many health professionals, really understand nutrition. Making sense of these nutrients is easier if you think that feeding your body is like baking a cake. Yes, a cake.

To turn out the way we want it to, a cake requires individual ingredients in the proper amounts. If you add too much of one ingredient, it affects the taste and even the appearance of the cake. If you add too little of another ingredient, the same thing happens. Now think about what would happen if we doubled all of our ingredients and tried to use the same pan. We would end up with a big, fat cake that hangs over our belts. Ooops…slip of the tongue, we meant baking pan. If we were to halve all of our ingredients, we would end up with a small, scrawny cake. That's not good either. In the case of our bodies, the "ingredients" that we put into them are the carbohydrates, fats, proteins, vitamins and minerals found in the food we eat.

Let's take this cake analogy a bit further. Water, carbohydrates, fats and proteins are the things that our bodies need the most of, just like milk, flour, butter, and eggs are the major ingredients of a cake. A cake also requires other ingredients, but in smaller amounts. Some are required by the tablespoon and others are required as a "pinch". Too little of these ingredients can also affect the cake. Likewise for vitamins and minerals. They may not be required by our bodies in the same amounts as carbohydrates, fats and proteins, but they are equally important for good health.

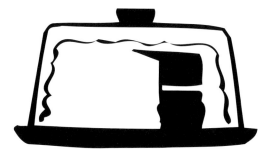

A quick word about vitamin and mineral supplements and fad diets. If we were baking a cake, most of us wouldn't add a tablespoon of an ingredient when the recipe called for a "pinch". Yet we load our bodies with megadoses of some vitamins and minerals because a so-called "health professional" tells us to. The same goes for loading up our bodies with high protein, high fat or high carbohydrate "fad" diets. It just doesn't make sense. When you read our sections on carbohydrates, fats, proteins, vitamins and minerals, keep in mind this analogy about baking a cake and if you forget everything else, please remember one thing.

Our diets, like our lives, should be *balanced*.

Carbohydrate Confusion

Now this is a subject that I can rant on about for hours!!! The dieticians and doctors who study nutrition tell us our total daily intake of calories must come from all types of food and that carbohydrates play an extremely important role in a balanced diet. But remember—all carbohydrates are not equal! After all, fruits and vegetables contain carbs and they pack high amounts of vitamins, minerals, antioxidants and fiber, and are proven to beat down all kinds of diseases, including cancer and heart disease. On the other hand, too much of some—especially carbohydrates with empty calories, like pop and candies or too much pasta—can lead to weight gain and other health problems. Just a little care in our choices, and we should strike a happy balance! Now let's hear from the doctors!

From the Doctors

We hear the term carbohydrate used all the time, but just what is a carbohydrate? Let's break down the word: carbo refers to carbon and hydrate refers to hydrogen and oxygen. Carbohydrates are molecules which contain carbon, hydrogen and oxygen in a specific ratio. Plants are the major manufacturers of carbohydrates.

Carbohydrates can be thought of as beads on a necklace. The individual beads are sugar molecules called monosaccharides (saccharide simply means sugar and mono means one). Glucose and fructose are the common monosaccharides (the –ose on the end of the words also means sugar). If you connect two beads, you can form other types of sugars called disaccharides (di means two). Sucrose, lactose and maltose are common types of disaccharides. Together, these two types of sugars are referred to as simple sugars. The following chart should make this much clearer:

Type of Simple Sugar	Common Name	Sources
1. Monosaccharides		
Glucose	Dextrose/blood sugar	Natural sugar in food
Fructose	Fruit sugar	Fruits and honey
2. Disaccharides		
Sucrose (glucose + fructose)	Table sugar, honey, maple syrup	Sugar beets, sugar cane, honey, maple syrup
Lactose (glucose + galactose)	Milk sugar	Dairy products
Maltose (glucose + glucose)	Malt sugar	Beer, cereals

Carbohydrate Confusion (cont.)

Sugar molecules can also combine in hundreds or thousands of beads to form the complex carbohydrates or polysaccharides. These act as the storage form of energy in plants and animals. In plants, this polysaccharide is referred to as starch while in animals it is called glycogen. Another type of complex carbohydrate is fiber which is only found in plants. The most common type of fiber is cellulose which makes up the structure of leaves, stems, seeds and fruit coverings and cannot be digested by humans.

Up until recently, people obtained their carbohydrates from eating fruits, grains and vegetables from a variety of sources including cereal grains, potatoes, legumes, lentils and rice. These foods were often high in complex carbohydrate and also provided fiber, vitamins and minerals. Although simple sugars can be found in many foods, good and bad for you, today people consume huge amounts of carbohydrates in the simple sugars found in candies, cakes, donuts, pop, etc. We refer to these as "empty calories" because the sugar in this case does not come from food which has all the nutrients found in fruits and vegetables; you just get the calories.

Carbohydrates account for about 40% to 50% of the typical North American diet today with half of this intake consisting of simple sugars. For the average person, this represents a yearly intake of around 60 pounds of table sugar and 45 pounds of corn syrup! Compare this to a hundred years ago when the yearly intake of simple sugars would have averaged around 5 pounds.

Because carbohydrates act as the primary source of energy for our bodies, we should strive to have carbohydrates supply 60% of our total calories, mostly in the form of unrefined fruits, grains and vegetables. During periods of increased physical activity, this should increase to 70%.

A little more on fiber. Most North Americans do not get nearly enough fiber in their diets. This is a result of a low intake of unprocessed fruits, grains and vegetables and a high intake of highly processed foods (which removes plant fiber) and a high intake of fiber-free animal products. High fiber intake may help decrease the risk of colon cancer. Certain types of fiber (water insoluble) found in rolled oats, oat bran, legumes, barley, brown rice, peas, carrots and a variety of fruits can lower a person's cholesterol.

Glycemic Index

The type of carbohydrates you eat can make a big difference. The rate at which the body breaks down carbohydrates into glucose varies from one food to another. You may have recently heard this rate referred to as the Glycemic Index or GI. It is measured on a scale of 1 to 100. Anything under 55 is a low GI. A GI over 70 is high.

Some low to medium GI foods are pasta, lentils and beans, skim milk, brown rice, nuts and seeds, whole grain breads and oatmeal, apples, blueberries, peaches and most fresh vegetables. They help you feel more satisfied.

High GI foods include soft drinks, cake and cookies, white bread, instant rice, white sugar, sweetened juices, fruit drinks, French fries, potato chips.

In general, the more refined the foods are, the higher the GI. So it's better to have an apple, than apple juice, whole wheat pasta instead of white pasta or instant rice.

Unclogging the Fat Information Highway

If there ever was a cause for confusion, it's the whole topic of fats! Some diet gurus insist we eliminate fat altogether, but as the doctors stress, fat is an important part of any healthy diet. Let's listen to them sort it out!

From the Doctors

Heart attacks are a major cause of death of men and women in North America. A heart attack usually occurs when the blood vessels (arteries) that carry blood and oxygen to the heart get clogged up or blocked with cholesterol deposits. Regular exercise and a diet low in fat can reduce our risk of having a heart attack. Now that we have your attention, let's try to clear up the confusion.

Before we talk about dietary fat, we should tell you a little about the cholesterol and triglycerides that circulate in our blood. Because of their importance in the development of heart attacks, tons of stuff has been written about these two substances. In order to understand this section and the danger of too much fat in the foods we eat, it's sufficient to know that there are microscopic, soft, waxy specks floating around in our bloodstream called "good" cholesterol (HDL) and "bad" cholesterol (LDL).

LDL is called "bad" cholesterol because it can build up on the walls of blood vessels, making them narrower or, in some cases, blocking them off completely. HDL is called "good" cholesterol because it collects and transports the extra cholesterol in the bloodstream to the liver where it is removed from the body. Triglycerides are another type of circulating fat that, if allowed to reach high levels, can also have an adverse effect on our health.

Dietary fat

The fat in the food we eat can be grouped into four categories – saturated fats, monounsaturated fats, polyunsaturated fats and trans – fats.

If you start to get confused about which fats are good and which are bad, have a look at our scale.

Unclogging the Fat Information Highway (cont.)

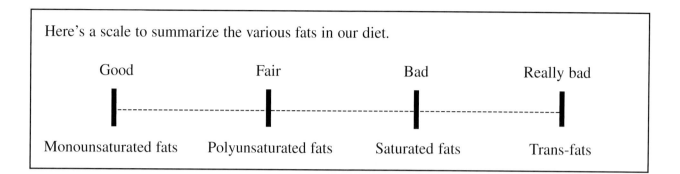

Here's a scale to summarize the various fats in our diet.

Good	Fair	Bad	Really bad
Monounsaturated fats	Polyunsaturated fats	Saturated fats	Trans-fats

Monounsaturated Fats

Monounsaturated fats are usually liquid at room temperature. Canola oil, olive oil and peanut oil are examples of monounsaturated fats. When you substitute saturated fats with monounsaturated fats in your diet, you decrease "bad" cholesterol (LDL) production.

Polyunsaturated Fats

Polyunsaturated fats are also usually liquid at room temperature. Examples include corn oil, safflower oil and sunflower oil. When you substitute saturated fats with polyunsaturated fats in your diet, they lower the body's production of "bad" cholesterol (LDL). But unfortunately, when compared to monounsaturated fats, they also lower the production of "good" cholesterol (HDL).

Saturated fats

Saturated fats are usually solid at room temperature and come mainly from animal sources, such as butter, cheese, high fat meats and lard. The tropical oils - coconut oil, palm oil and palm kernel oil - are also high in saturated fats. A diet high in saturated fats increases the body's production of "bad" cholesterol (LDL). Conversely, a diet low in saturated fats decreases the body's production of "bad" cholesterol (LDL).

Trans-Fats

A word about "trans – fats". Trans - fats are made during food manufacturing by a process called "hydrogenation". Like saturated fats, these fats raise "bad" cholesterol (LDL). They also lower "good" cholesterol (HDL), making them even worse than saturated fats. Major sources of trans – fats include crackers, cookies, donuts, french fries and fried chicken.

Should all fat be eliminated from our diet?

No. Fats are an important part of a healthy diet. Dietary fats are an excellent source of energy, especially for young children. Fats are important for absorption of the fat soluble vitamins and are used to manufacture hormones and to build healthy cells. Dietary fats should be limited to 30% of our total calories, not eliminated from our diet. No more than 10% of our food calories should come from a combination of saturated fats and trans-fats.

Sandi's Tips

So you see, it isn't complicated. Simply replace corn oil or vegetable oil with canola or olive oil and you're already lowering your production of "bad" cholesterol (LDL). Since fat should make up 30 percent of our calories, for the average woman that equates to about 65 grams; for the average man 90 grams. I try to choose lower-fat dairy products, leaner meats and food prepared with little or no fat. I've also been getting extra cautious when I see "partially hydrogenated oil" on the ingredients list for foods, because now I know it contains some trans-fat. Since they are the worst kind, according to doctors, I'm trying to cut them out. Oh, and by the way, did you know that a large order of fast-food fries or a frosted donut by itself can put you over the daily limit for trans-fat?!!!

On another note, you've heard about Omega-3 fatty acids, most of which, though not all, fall into the monounsaturated fats category, the good ones. Omega-3s are found primarily in fatty fish such as salmon and haddock. Other sources are sardines, mackerel, scallops, tuna, broccoli, kale, spinach, canola, flaxseed and soybean oils. There is research showing that Omega-3s may offer protection against heart disease and other medical conditions.

When You Think of Protein, Think Building Blocks

From the Doctors

As we already mentioned in the "medical gobbledygook" section, we had a hard time determining what to say about proteins. We find proteins fascinating and we wanted to explain everything about them, from how they are made, to how they are digested, to where they come from. Our editorial team suggested that we keep it simple and concentrate on telling people what proteins do for us. We came up with a compromise - we would use another analogy to explain proteins. So here it goes…

Most of us have played with children's building blocks. Proteins are made up of individual building blocks called amino acids. When we eat protein in food, our body breaks the protein down into these building blocks. Our body contains blueprints which enable it to reassemble the building blocks into the proteins that we require. These proteins can be used in a variety of ways. Many form the structural framework for tissues like bone, hair and skin or our internal organs. Others have specialized functions, like transporting oxygen in the bloodstream or building muscle. Proteins are also an essential part of our immune and hormonal systems.

Proteins are important for everything. In fact, without any protein in our body, we'd end up as a puddle on the floor!!! Fortunately, the average North American diet is relatively high in protein, so most of us will never have a problem getting enough.

Chicken, fish, eggs and red meat are all excellent sources of dietary protein. Once we get the "building blocks" inside our bodies, we can start to build and build and build. Because of all this building, we need a constant supply of dietary protein. We can't store proteins like we can store fat.

Vegetarians who don't eat food from animal sources must take special care to ensure that they get enough protein, and the right kinds of protein in their diet. They must eat a wide variety of different plant foods and lots of them. Tofu is an excellent addition to a vegetarian diet because it is a source of high quality protein.

Health experts recommend around 15% of our total calories come from protein. However, the recommended amount of dietary protein can vary with people's age and their level of activity. With the exception of vegetarians, most North Americans will consume more than double the required amount of protein, every day. So…for most of us, additional protein in the form of supplements is unnecessary.

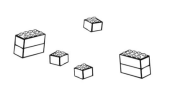

The "Let's Just Take a Vitamin Pill" Era

Vitamins are an essential part of our diet. They are found naturally in food and play an important role in normal body function. Most people can get all the vitamins they need from a well balanced diet. Fresh fruits and vegetables are nutritional powerhouses and are an excellent source of vitamins. Unlike a vitamin pill, fruits and vegetables also contain fiber and other nutrients that are important for good health.

There are 13 well known vitamins. Vitamins A, D, E, and K are called "fat-soluble" vitamins. Your body is able to store these vitamins in large amounts for long periods of time. Vitamin C and the B-complex vitamins are examples of "water soluble" vitamins. These vitamins can only be stored in small amounts and you must continually replenish your body's supply. Any excess "water soluble" vitamins that you consume end up in your "pee". Buying and taking mega doses of these vitamins simply gives you expensive urine.

We are going to take you on a Safari through the jungle of vitamins and minerals

We want people to be clear about a couple things. First, vitamin *deficiencies* are rare in North America. However, some people may have minor vitamin shortages. These may include people on certain types of diets, people with particular food allergies or those who are lactose intolerant. Vegetarians (especially vegans) may have shortages or vitamin deficiencies because they restrict their intake of some foods. We want to emphasize that the vast majority of North Americans can get their vitamins from a well balanced diet. We don't need megavitamins. Second, despite all the hype, there is nothing "magical" about vitamins. They are simply nutrients just like carbohydrates, fats, proteins and minerals. Vitamins get a lot of attention because they can be packaged, promoted and sold with little risk to the buying public. While some people may benefit from vitamin supplementation, the majority of people do not.

Keep in mind that vitamin supplements can be expensive. We suggest that you invest your money instead in good nutrition. A well balanced diet, including lots of fresh fruits and vegetables, will allow people to get the vitamins they need without having to take a pill. The chart below explains the foods that are good sources of fat soluble and water soluble vitamins.

Water-Soluble Vitamins

Vitamin	a.k.a.	Dietary Sources
Vitamin B_1	Thiamine	Pork, organ meats, whole grains, legumes
Vitamin B_2	Riboflavin	Widely distributed in foods
Vitamin B_6	Pyridoxine	Meats, vegetables, whole-grain cereals
Vitamin B_{12}	Cyanocobalamin	Muscle meats, eggs, dairy products, (absent in plant foods)
Biotin		Legumes, vegetables, meats
Vitamin C	Ascorbic acid	Citrus fruits, tomatoes, green and red peppers, salad greens
Folate	Folic Acid	Legumes, green vegetables, whole-wheat products
Niacin	Nicotinic Acid	Liver, lean meats, grains, legumes (can be formed from tryptophan)
Pantothenate	Pantothenic acid	Widely distributed in foods

The "Let's Just Take a Vitamin Pill" Era (cont.)

Fat-Soluble Vitamins

Vitamin	a.k.a	Dietary Sources
Vitamin A	Retinol	Provitamin A (betacarotene) widely distributed in green vegetables Retinol present in milk, butter, cheese, fortified margarine
Vitamin D	Calciferol	Cod-liver oil, eggs, dairy products, fortified milk, and margarine
Vitamin E	Tocopherol	Seeds, green leafy vegetables, margarines, shortenings
Vitamin K	K vitamin group	Green leafy vegetables, small amount in cereals, fruits, and meats

Major Minerals

Mineral	Dietary Sources
Calcium	Milk, cheese, dark green vegetables, dried legumes
Phosphorus	Milk, cheese, yogurt, meat, poultry, grains, fish
Potassium	Leafy vegetables, cantelope, lima beans, potatoes, bananas, milk, meats, coffee, tea
Sulfur	Obtained as part of dietary protein, and present in food preservatives
Sodium	Common salt
Chlorine (chloride)	Part of salt-containing food. Some vegetables and fruits
Magnesium	Whole grains, green leafy vegetables

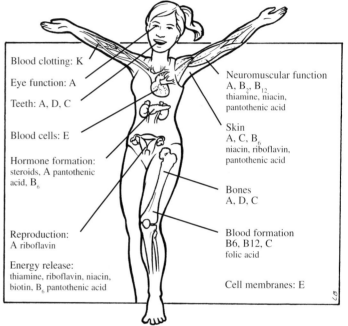

Water Soluble and Fat Soluble Vitamins

Minerals

Minerals are a little different than vitamins. Minerals come from the earth; they cannot be "manufactured" by plants or animals. But we don't have to eat rocks and dirt to get our minerals. So how do we get them? Simple, minerals are found in the earth, plants take up the minerals, animals eat the plants and we eat plants and the meat from animals.

Some minerals are required in very large amounts. They are called "major" minerals. Others are required in smaller amounts. They are called "trace" minerals. Calcium and phosphorus are examples of major minerals that are required by the body, in significant amounts, to make bone. The chart below explains the foods that are good sources of major and trace minerals. Like vitamins, there is nothing "magical" about minerals; however, our bodies need them in adequate amounts for various functions.

Trace Minerals

Mineral	Dietary Sources
Fluorine	Drinking water, tea, seafood
Zinc	Widely distributed in foods
Copper	Meats, drinking water
Selenium	Seafood, meat, grains
Iron	Eggs, lean meats, legumes, whole grains, green leafy vegetables
Iodine (Iodide)	Marine fish and shellfish, dairy products, vegetables, iodized salt
Chromium	Legumes, cereals, organ meats, fats, vegetable oils, meats, whole grains

Don't Pee Your Bones Down the Drain!

If I hear one more prominent celebrity profess to the world that North Americans don't need to consume dairy products, I'm going to screeeeeeeam! I am now going to use this opportunity to tell anyone who fits this mold to get a grip and fully understand the impact they're having on kids, BEFORE they speak! In a nutshell, milk is a convenient, economical way for children, teens and adults to get calcium in their diet. Celebrities compare our culture to other cultures which don't consume dairy products, yet have low levels of osteoporosis. What they don't tell you is that those cultures often obtain their calcium from non-dairy sources. We have taken dairy products out of our diet but haven't replaced them with an adequate source of calcium. Unfortunately, in many cases, kids have replaced milk with soda pop. The phosphates in the drinks actually bind to calcium and it gets peed out of our bodies. I meet thousands of teenage girls and guys, trying so hard to be like their celebrity advocates and what they don't get is this…these celebrities often have highly paid trainers and advisors to help them get their calcium from other sources. So let's get real here. The average family can't afford such a luxury. But don't believe me, let's ask the doctors...

From the Doctors

Adults lose calcium from their bones as part of the normal aging process. Losing *too much* calcium can result in abnormal thinning of the bones called osteoporosis. Therefore it is vital to build as much bone as possible during your youth. It would surprise many parents to learn that the period of maximum bone-building for girls occurs between the ages of 11 to 13 and for boys between the ages of 13 to 15! Even more surprising is that up to 25% of your total adult bone is built during this two-year period. This amount represents as much bone as most people will lose in their entire adult life!

Sooo…it is very important for children to consume enough calcium throughout their childhood and adolescence to help build and maintain healthy bones.

Here's some bad news: Lots of kids are not getting enough calcium. Only about 25% of boys and 10% of girls ages 9 to 17 actually meet the recommended intake levels. In the good old days, dairy products provided 75% of the dietary calcium. Unfortunately kids today often replace milk with soft drinks during the time of maximum bone building, resulting in too little calcium intake when it is needed the most. Recent evidence shows that a high intake of carbonated beverages, especially cola drinks, may increase the risk of bone fractures in teen girls.

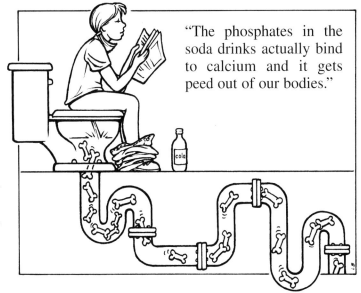

"The phosphates in the soda drinks actually bind to calcium and it gets peed out of our bodies."

Many foods are very good sources of calcium and kids should be encouraged to include them in their diet on a daily basis. Not all children like or tolerate dairy products so these kids must consume alternate sources of calcium, such as calcium-fortified soy or rice beverages, calcium-fortified natural fruit juices, dark green leafy vegetables and canned fish such as salmon. For some children, calcium supplementation may also be needed.

Don't forget, our bodies need Vitamin D to absorb calcium. Vitamin D is produced when our skin is exposed to the sun. However, in the winter, it can be difficult to get enough sun exposure, especially in Northern climates. While we encourage its use, sunscreen can prevent Vitamin D from being made by the skin. The great news is that adequate amounts of Vitamin D can easily be obtained from Vitamin D-fortified dairy products, egg yolks, tuna, salmon and liver.

Weight-bearing activities where your bones and muscles work against gravity, are also required to build strong healthy bones. Examples include brisk walking, jump rope, dancing, gymnastics, and activities that involve running, such as jogging, soccer and tennis. Resistance or strength training are also good ways to build and maintain healthy bones.

Adequate Intake Level (AI) for Calcium	
Age and life stage group	Calcium (mg/day)
0-6 months	210
7-12 months	270
1-3 years	500
4-8 years	800
9-18 years	1,300
19-50 years	1,000
51 years and older	1,200
Pregnancy or breastfeeding	1,500

All this bone building stuff pays off. If you're a teen and you plan on being an active adult, following this advice will allow you to enjoy your activities without worrying about a higher risk of fractures or osteoporosis down the road. Women in particular are at risk for osteoporosis and they should make sure they get enough calcium, Vitamin D and weight-bearing activity.

Calcium Content of Some Foods

Food	Serving	Elemental Calcium (mg)	Estimated Absorbable Calcium (mg)	Servings needed to equal 8 oz of milk
Milk	8 ounces	300	96	1.0
Yogurt	8 ounces	300	96	1.0
Cheddar cheese	1.5 ounces	303	97	1.0
Chinese cabbage	1/2 cup, cooked	239	95	1.0
Tofu, calcium set	1/2 cup	258	80	1.2
Broccoli	1/2 cup, cooked	35	22	4.5
Rhubarb	1/2 cup, cooked	174	10	9.5
Red beans	1/2 cup, cooked	41	10	9.7
Spinach	1/2 cup, cooked	115	6	16.3
Almonds, dry roasted	1/2 cup, 250 mL	189	17	5.6
Sesame seeds	1 oz, 25 g	280	8	12
Sesame seeds, toasted	1 oz, 25 g	280	37	2.5
Non-dairy soy milks	1 cup, 250 mL	300	24-62	1.5-4

Sandi's Tips

Get a good look at the calcium content chart - it shows that you have to eat a backyard of spinach to equal a glass of milk! But hey, getting calcium in your diet may be easier than you think. Here are a few changes you can make. Toasted sesame seeds are loaded with calcium…toss them on everything you can, soups, stir fries, toast, cereal, you name it! Vanilla yogurt is still my favorite fruit dip. Fruit smoothies with yogurt or tofu are amazing…even my yogurt hater dies for them. (See "Importance of Breakfast" for recipe.). Get some chocolate syrup for milk if the kids like that as a treat drink. If they aren't having soda pop and are opting for chocolate milk…what the heck!

Our Society: A Lack of Balance

From the Doctors

It's hard these days not to pick up the paper or turn on the TV and hear something about how people in North America are becoming increasingly overweight and inactive. We're told that as a society we are eating too much of the wrong kind of food and spending too little time being physically active. Well, unfortunately, that's pretty close to the truth. It's not hard to understand why this is happening. Food has now become an industrial product and high fat/high energy food is readily available and cheap. A multi-billion dollar food industry advertising campaign exposes our children to thousands of food ads every year, convincing them to eat food which is bad for them.

Activity-wise, North American society has changed a lot in the last 50 years. It has become increasingly automated (we don't even have to open most doors) and many physical labor-type jobs are now done by a machine while we sit and "supervise". Much of our leisure time is now spent in sedentary activities like watching videos, playing computer games or surfing the net. It is estimated that 40 years ago kids spent 400 percent more energy than kids today.

The Energy Balance

Our society is out of balance. A massive increase in the calories in the food we eat (energy in) with a significant decrease in physical activity (energy out) has tipped the scales towards obesity and all its resulting health consequences.

It Is Not All About Fat

On the other side of the coin is another huge problem. Our society has decided, largely through the media, that the "ideal" body size is extremely thin, a size impossible to achieve for the vast majority of people. Society has made fatness something to be ashamed of, but provides easier ways to get fat! This has especially affected women, including young girls, and leads to what some have described as a "disturbed" relationship with food. As a result we find really young girls dieting and possibly developing an eating disorder. It's a vicious and unhealthy cycle.

Obesity has a strong genetic component. Everyone has a pre-programmed body size, much like height or hair color. People who attain their "natural" size through a reasonable diet and an adequate level of physical activity are healthy. Heavier-set, but fit people are healthier than thin, sedentary people. In other words, an inactive lifestyle is probably a greater risk factor for many diseases than mild obesity.

It's all about balance. If you adopt a lifestyle where you eat and exercise in a reasonable way, you stand a great chance of being healthy. It's not about converting to some fad diet or exercise program but about realizing that, although we can't change society, we can change the way we live our lives in society. For our kids to be healthy adults, we need to teach them this simple lesson and act as their role models!

Benefits of Activity

From the Doctors

> - Reduces the risk of developing many different diseases
> - Increases endurance, flexibility, and muscle strength
> - Reduces body fat and builds bone mass
> - Increases self-esteem and the feeling of well-being while lowering stress
> - Decreases cigarette use and other deviant behaviors in youth

The Link to Self Esteem

Our self-esteem can really affect the lifestyle choices we make. This is especially true for teenagers. Low self-esteem is associated with depression, eating disorders, delinquency, suicide and many other adolescent problems. Most kids are hung up on their physical appearance (weren't we???). We live in a society where even mild obesity is often a cause for self-criticism leading to a feeling of decreased self-worth. This makes regular exercise and proper nutrition a must for everyone, not only those who struggle with their weight.

We also know that physical activity leads to a feeling of well-being, so you get a double portion of good vibes from being active! We should encourage our kids to be active with the friends they hang out with, whether it's skateboarding, picking up a game of tennis at the local tennis court, or being part of a sports team. "Hanging" with inactive kids who eat poorly and are critical of healthy lifestyles often means adopting this way of thinking to fit in. If we notice this is happening, we have to work even harder to emphasize to our kids the importance of healthy living. Parents often underestimate the huge influence they have. Certainly peer pressure exerts influence, but even though we go through phases with our kids, in the long run, we have a big impact on the way they think. It is especially important to lead by example.

Stress also plays a major role in all our lives. Again, regular exercise and good eating help reduce stress and allow us to cope better when it rears its ugly head.

The Risks of Inactivity

A sedentary lifestyle is a major risk factor for many illnesses and may represent the same risk as cigarette smoking!

- High blood pressure
- High cholesterol
- Diabetes
- Respiratory disorders
- Osteoporosis (thinning of the bones)
- Heart disease
- Stroke
- Obesity

Activity 101

I've had some huge struggles with exercise, too! I made a decision to stop listening to all the fitness experts who'd tell me that if I didn't work out for at least 20 minutes, I wasn't burning off a thing. This drove me to do nothing! I figured 10 minutes to get ready, at least 20 minutes to work out, and then another 20 minutes to clean up after sweating. That's almost one hour and, in my life, I just didn't have an extra hour. When I told myself that five minutes away from the phone and the kids was good for my head, things changed. All the excuses why I couldn't leave (you know, the laundry, I had a hard day, if I didn't have an excuse, I would simply create one), were all of a sudden easy to ignore because after all, I was only going for five minutes. A funny thing happens once you're out there away from the kids and the phones, and you realize you don't need to go back quite yet!!! If we can encourage our non-athletically-inclined children to do the same, just watch what happens. Now here's some scientific know-how from the doctors…

From the Doctors

It seems just about every time you turn on the TV, look in a magazine, or go on-line, you are exposed to people promoting some kind of exercise program. It's really hard to sort out the science from the hype. Let's try and simplify the whole exercise thing.

Exercise is really only a structured form of physical activity and physical activity is just using your muscles to move your body and expend energy in the process. Every time the word "exercise" appears in this book, you can easily replace it with the term "physical activity". This is one of the beautiful things about the body: we use energy whether we are raking the grass, climbing a flight of stairs or playing a sport.

Our muscles need energy for us to be physically active. They can use carbohydrates (sugars), fats and proteins as fuel. The type of fuel used depends on how long and hard we exercise, what our nutritional status is, and a whole bunch of other things. The key is that we burn calories whenever we are physically active.

You don't have to be a jock to undertake and enjoy physical activity. It's not always about playing sports or going to the gym. Many people do not feel comfortable in these environments and choose not to be physically active. What's the solution to this problem?

Getting started

This is really the simplest part of all, yet often the hardest to accomplish. You just have to decide to incorporate physical activity as a routine part of your day, whether you are a stay-at-home mom, an executive, or someone who works shift work. Physical activity doesn't have to be totally exhausting to improve your health, it just has to be regular.

Walk whenever possible. Use the stairs instead of the escalator or elevator. Get off the bus early. Park your car as far away as possible from the doors at the mall. Walk the dog. Play with your kids in a physically active way. Dust off the bike.

How much is enough?

The amount of time you need to spend being physically active to improve your health depends on the intensity of the activity. The key is to build up slowly. Many people make the mistake of hurting themselves by going at it way too hard at the beginning and quickly losing interest. You need to choose a variety of activities so you don't get bored and you need to do things that you want to do and not what you think you should do. If you don't like running, don't run! It can also be helpful to find an exercise partner to help keep you motivated.

If you're just starting, it is recommended you spend 60 minutes a day being physically active. 60 minutes a day, you gasp! Well, this is way easier than you think. You simply need to accumulate 60 minutes in a day by being active for periods of at least 10 minutes. As the intensity of your activity increases, the time you need to spend being physically active to maintain good health actually decreases. At a moderate to vigorous level of activity, you only need to accumulate 30 minutes a day for 4 days a week, but everyone is strongly encouraged to be active every day.

Here's an example of how to get your 60 minutes in during a day. Stretch for 10 minutes in the car or while sitting at work, walk at lunch for 20 minutes, cut the grass for 20 minutes, and do some sit-ups and pushups for 10 minutes. There's your 60 minutes!

Time needed depends on effort

Light Effort *60 minutes*	**Moderate Effort** *30-60 minutes*	**Vigorous Effort** *20-30 minutes*
• Light walking	• Brisk walking	• Aerobics
• Volleyball	• Biking	• Jogging
• Easy gardening	• Raking leaves	• Hockey
• Stretching	• Swimming	• Basketball
	• Dancing	• Fast swimming
	• Water aerobics	• Fast dancing

> How does it feel?
> How warm am I?
> What is my breathing like?

• Starting to feel warm	• Warmer	• Quite warm
• Slight increase in breathing rate	• Greater increase in breathing rate	• More out of breath

Range needed to stay healthy

From Canada's Physical Activity Guide to Healthy Active Living

How hard do I need to exercise?

The above chart gave some ideas on how to estimate your effort level. Another way to help measure how hard you are exercising is by using your heart rate. Simply take 220 and minus your age to obtain your maximum heart rate (the rate you should never exceed when exercising). You should exercise at between 50% and 75% of your maximum heart rate. You can determine what your heart rate is while exercising by taking your pulse (use your index and middle finger to feel the pulse in your neck just below your jaw), count the number of beats in 10 seconds and multiply it by 6. This gives your heart rate in beats per minute.

Example: If you are 40 years old, then your maximum heart rate is 220 – 40 = 180 beats per minute. Then multiply this by both 50% and 75% to find your target heart rate zone. In this case it would be 90 to 135 beats per minute.

How hard do I need to exercise? (cont.)

You can also purchase a heart rate monitor to wear on your wrist and automatically measure your heart rate. A less accurate way to determine your effort level is to use the "talk test". If you're so out of breath, you are unable to finish a short sentence without taking a breath, you're exercising too hard.

If you're just starting an exercise program, begin at 50% of your maximum heart rate and work your way up slowly over the next few months to 75%. Again, slow and steady is the best approach.

What types of activities should I do?

There are three basic kinds of activity we need to participate in to stay healthy: endurance activities, flexibility activities, and strength activities.

Endurance activities help strengthen the heart and lungs (cardiorespiratory fitness). These activities are continuous, such as running, swimming, biking or mowing the grass, and should be done 4 to 7 days a week.

Flexibility helps muscles, tendons and joints function in an ideal way and can help prevent injuries. These include activities which involve stretching and bending, such as dance, gymnastics, Tai Chi and yoga. You should do these activities 4 to 7 days a week.

Strengthening activities help build strong muscles and bones. Strength training involves making muscles stronger, which differs from weight training where the goal is to make muscles bigger. Bigger is not always better. Strength exercises can use weights or weight machines but also include activities such as climbing, lifting and carrying your children or groceries or doing some pushups. This type of activity should be done 2 to 4 days a week.

"I don't have enough time to exercise."

We can all build regular physical activity into our lives - we just have to want to do it. As you can see, it doesn't take a ton of money, effort or special equipment or facilities to get enough physical activity to improve and maintain our health.

Should I be worried about starting an exercise program?

Most people can exercise safely. If you are not used to physical activity, start slowly and gradually build up. Remember, the aim is to be healthy, not to lose a whole bunch of weight in a real short period of time. If you have a history of heart disease, lung disease, diabetes, high blood pressure, problems with your joints or another medical concern, you should talk with your doctor before increasing your level of activity. This is also true if you are pregnant or breastfeeding.

Much like changing to a healthier diet, the goal of becoming physically active is to make a permanent change in your lifestyle which then becomes a habit. Fad diets and exercise programs usually fail because people are not able to adopt these changes in the long run.

Leading a healthy life is not hard work, it's just steady work. And spoil yourself sometimes, too! Take a day now and then just to "veg" out on the couch with your favorite movies and enjoy that chocolate sundae.

Stretching and Why!

Stretching is actually a type of exercise. It can be as simple as bending down to touch your toes or a formalized activity such as yoga. Stretching is used to improve the body's flexibility.

Some people are naturally more flexible than others. This is often because their joints, tendons and ligaments have a different type of chemical structure. Everyone can remember the super-flexible kid who was "double-jointed" or could do the splits. Another group of people tend to be rather inflexible or tight. As well, we tend to become less flexible as we age, or following an injury, or if we become sedentary and do not ever stretch our muscles.

Flexibility is determined by the "stretchiness" of our muscles, skin, ligaments and joints. Stretching helps improve the flexibility of all these structures.

Why Should We Stretch?

Good question. Flexibility appears to play an important role in preventing injury, during both daily activity and while participating in sports, dance and general fitness training. In fact, regular use of muscles during exercise, without stretching, can lead to decreased flexibility. Stretching is crucial to make sure flexibility is maintained. As well, flexibility is required to maximize performance during complicated movements which are required when participating in many sports, like throwing a baseball, kicking a ball in soccer or during a dance routine.

When Should We Stretch?

Muscles, joints and tendons prefer to be stretched when they are warm. This makes sense if you think of an elastic band. You can always stretch a warm elastic band further than a cold one before it snaps (ouch!). A warm-up to increase the blood flow to your muscles is ideal and is as easy as a light 5-minute jog or bike ride. You can then stretch before your workout, after your workout or both.

How Should We Stretch?

Proper stretching technique is also very important. Improper stretching may cause an injury. As mentioned earlier, do not stretch a cold muscle. As well, stretching should always be painless. Stretching to the point of producing pain can cause an injury to the muscle, joint, etc. and the pain itself actually triggers the muscle to tighten. To stretch properly, begin slowly until you feel a gentle, pain-free pulling sensation in the muscle. Then hold the stretch for at least 20 to 30 seconds and repeat 2 or 3 times. "Bouncing" while you stretch is not really of any benefit and can lead to injury. Within reason, there is no limit to the number of times you can stretch in a day. If you are just starting a stretching program, be patient. Increasing flexibility takes lots of time and effort. If you exercise on a regular basis, remember stretching is an important part of any complete exercise program.

Physical therapists and other fitness professionals are often very good at teaching people a variety of stretches for all parts of the body and will also make sure you're doing the stretches properly. It's often worth a visit if you are not sure you're doing the right stretches or are unsure of your technique.

Sometimes aggressive stretching following certain types of injuries is harmful. An example of this is if you suffer a badly bruised thigh. If in doubt, talk to your doctor or therapist.

Childhood Activity 101

From the Doctors

Parents frequently ask us, as sport medicine physicians, what types of physical activities are safe for kids to participate in. This is a topic as confusing as dieting and exercise fads.

In general, a physical activity program should help us improve and maintain endurance, flexibility and strength.

Endurance activities help strengthen the heart and lungs (cardio-respiratory fitness).

Flexibility helps muscles, tendons and joints function in an ideal way and can help prevent injuries.

Strengthening activities help build strong muscles and bones.

QUESTION: Which of the above activities are safe for kids?

ANSWER: All of them!

Here are the answers to a few common questions parents frequently ask:

Can kids strength train safely?

Generally, yes. Using free weights and machines to increase strength appears not to pose a significant risk of injury to kids. Supervision by qualified individuals to ensure proper lifting technique is very important. Children should not attempt to lift their maximum weight (the most they can lift just once) before their growth plates close (so-called skeletal maturity), due to the risk of growth plate injury. They should also avoid rapid maneuvers (like the snatch or the clean and jerk performed by Olympic weight lifters), power lifting (three maximum lifts) and bodybuilding. Don't forget, strength training is used to increase muscle strength, not build bigger muscles. This means doing many repetitions (13-15) of low-to-moderate weight and increasing the resistance or weight gradually as strength improves (by 5 to 10%). Strength gains of 30 to 50% can be obtained by kids despite the fact their muscles often don't get any bigger! Remember, strength training is only one part of a well-balanced fitness program.

Can kids participate in long distance running?

Again, generally yes. Running does not seem to harm young joints or growth plates and some experts believe kids can even compete in long distance running. Just remember, kids have less tolerance to heat stress and this always needs to be monitored closely.

Should kids use nutritional supplements to enhance performance?

Use of these supplements by kids is strongly discouraged for a variety of reasons. A healthy diet is always the best way to maximize performance.

Are plyometrics safe for kids?

Plyometrics are specific types of jumping, hopping and throwing exercises that link strength with speed of movement to produce power.

When properly supervised, plyometrics are safe for children prior to puberty. They can also help build strong bone.

What about "no pain, no gain" when kids are exercising?

"No pain, no gain" should never be applied to kids and they should not train through injuries. At the same time, complete rest from training may not be necessary or practical. A modified program, where the child is able to continue to train, but also avoid those activities which could prevent healing of their injury, is often the best. Advice should be sought from the appropriate health care professional who can often be referred by the coach.

Just remember, children are not miniature adults:

1. Children have less endurance when exercising than adults, but generally recover more quickly ("Let's do it again, Mommy!").

2. No single sport or exercise regimen is uniquely beneficial for the physical or emotional well-being of children. It's most important to find various activities that will be interesting for the child and are appropriate to his or her age and physical abilities.

3. If parents have any concerns about their kids participating in certain types of exercise programs, they should always discuss this with their family doctor or pediatrician.

The Competitive Child Athlete

From the Doctors

Although many concerns surround intense competition in children, little scientific information either supports or disproves certain risks that these growing athletes may face. We'll deal with these risks one by one.

Musculoskeletal (muscle, bone and joint) injury and growth

Young athletes, with the help of their coaches and parents, must train at a level that allows them to maximize their performance while avoiding injury. However, certain types of repetitive training in the growing athlete may cause injuries to growth plates, joints and the developing spine. For example, gymnasts who repeatedly hyper-extend their backs can develop stress fractures in their lower spine.

Nutrition

Proper nutrition is critical for both good health and optimal sports performance. Nutritional requirements are often increased by both training and the growth process of young athletes.

> **Typical areas of concern include:**
> a. Adequate total caloric (energy) intake
> b. Balanced diet
> c. Iron intake
> d. Calcium intake

Puberty

Some highly-trained female athletes start their periods 1 to 2 years after the average girl. This may be related to under-nutrition, training stress or low percentage of body fat. However, the girls who often are selected to compete at a high level in these sports have body types which are characterized by narrow hips, slender physiques, long legs and low body fat. The girls with this body type often start their periods later than other girls, regardless of activity level.

The timing of puberty in boys is not affected by intense training. As well, it has not been proven that intensive training in boys or girls will affect their adult height.

Following puberty, certain highly trained girls may be at risk of developing the "female athlete triad". This triad consists of: 1. infrequent or absent periods after normal periods have started; 2. abnormal thinning of the bones (osteoporosis); 3. disordered eating. This is a serious problem that must be dealt with by a physician.

Psychological Development

Despite the fears of physical and emotional burnout related to the stress and anxiety of training and competing at an elite level, these problems are actually seen in a small percentage of competitive young athletes. Most kids find this type of training and competition a positive experience.

Research does show, however, that children who avoid competing in a single sport until reaching puberty tend to be more consistent performers, have fewer injuries and compete longer than those who specialize at an early age.

Dangers in Drinks

While doing the research for this book, I was shocked to find out how much of what we drink contributes to the problem of obesity. Sounds unbelievable, doesn't it? But let me share some statistics with you.

Over the past 20 years, soft drink guzzling has soared, and intake of milk and 100% unsweetened fruit juice has taken a dive. One real problem is that most sweetened drinks, and this includes iced teas, lemonades, fruit drinks and specialty coffees, are loaded with lots of calories but very little else of nutritional value. This can lead to inadequate consumption of key nutrients like folate, vitamin A, vitamin C and calcium. There is a real concern that kids are not getting enough calcium in the prime bone-building years. This trend starts in early preschool and by the time kids reach teen years, one quarter of them are downing MORE THAN 26 ounces of soda pop a day! It is becoming very clear that increased soda pop consumption is contributing to childhood obesity.

We wonder why our kids are caught in the soft drink trap. Well, maybe this will help you to understand. One nationally advertised soft drink has a marketing budget in the area of 100 million dollars! Compare this to the government-sponsored campaign organized to increase our intake of fruits and vegetables which had a marketing budget of 700 thousand dollars.

It's not just the millions of dollars in advertising on TV that gets us replacing healthy drinks with soda pop. In this time of decreased educational funding, schools have been lured by soda companies which provide extra funding to schools for programs, in return for exclusive rights to market their product. This has made soda pop both accessible and acceptable.

How Much is Enough?

Have you seen the size of drinks these days? You could park a truck in some of those cups!!! The most popular convenience stores and fast food joints offer big deals on oversized portions of soda pop to make you think you're getting better value. A large drink costs only a few cents more than a smaller one. These larger drinks can deliver more than 600 calories without actually giving a feeling of satisfying our hunger. That's the equivalent of a quarter cup of sugar! YUCK!!!

Overall, Americans are consuming 40% more soda pop than they were in 1978 and are now spending $54 billion a year on it! (Is it merely coincidental that the rise in childhood and adult obesity has risen accordingly during the same period of time?)

So, I will just drink diet soda pop instead, right? Remember, calories are only one of the problems with soda pop. Diet pop is still replacing nutritious unsweetened fruit juices and calcium-rich milk in our diet.

Wonderful Water

One easy step towards a healthier life is replacing soda pop and sweetened drinks with water.

Here are a few reasons to get hooked on water

- Water boosts your energy.
- Water helps you think better... It actually plays a role in transmission of messages within the brain and from the brain to the muscles.
- Water lubricates moving body parts.
- Try water instead of a headache pill. You will be suprised how often dehydration is causing the headache.
- Remember, if you wait until you are thirsty you're already dehydrated. So drink water and drink it often, at least six to eight 8 oz glasses per day.

I know the doctors are just chomping at the bit to talk about this one...hit it guys!

From the Doctors

The human body is made up mostly of water. In fact, 50 to 70% is made up of good old H_2O. Exactly how much of the body is made up of water depends on a person's age, sex and body composition. Muscle contains more water than fat. For this reason a 25-year-old athlete's body will have more water than a 50-year-old non-athlete. Women naturally have more body fat than men and accordingly they have less water in their bodies. What really matters is that you get enough water in your body to stay healthy and not get dehydrated. Water is so important that, without it, we would die within a matter of days.

Good sources of water and not so good sources of water

We agree with Sandi about the benefits of plain old water. Listen to this---every time we breathe, sweat or go to the bathroom, we lose water. Because of this, we need to be constantly providing our bodies with water. The best source of water is...water. Most parts of North America have good drinking water straight from the tap. Areas that don't have good tap water may need to drink filtered or bottled water.

Other good sources of water include milk, unsweetened fruit juices, herbal tea and raw fruits and vegetables.

Dangers in Drinks (cont.)

Keep in mind that while soft drinks and sport drinks are sources of water, there are some drawbacks. Next to water, sugar is the main component of most of these drinks and, while there are other factors that contribute to obesity, a constant supply of sugar in our drinking water doesn't help. If North Americans continue to consume high calorie "drinks" and then maintain their nutrients through the calories from food, well… you can do the math. Some sport drinks contain a lot of sodium, potassium and chloride. While these substances are important for our bodies, most North Americans get enough in their diets so they shouldn't have them in their drinking water. Sport drinks are okay for people participating in endurance sports, but for everyday consumption, water is still best.

The caffeine in tea and coffee is a diuretic (a chemical that makes your kidneys filter out water from the bloodstream). As a result you lose more water (in the form of urine) than you would if you just drank plain H_2O. For this reason, tea, coffee, and other caffeinated beverages are not great choices to keep hydrated. Incidentally, the alcohol in beer, wine and spirits also acts as a diuretic. For obvious reasons, not many health professionals recommend substituting your daily drinking water with alcoholic beverages.

> **When you want to replace the fluids that you lose on a daily basis, plain old water is still the best choice.**

Sandi's Tips

- Don't completely forbid soda pop and other sweetened beverages, because that will make them all the more desirable. Just make healthier choice drinks available most of the time.

- Keep water within easy reach and keep it cold. You can keep it in the fridge, use a water filter, or get a home water cooler. You will be amazed how this will increase your family's water intake.

- If your child is not allergic to milk but just doesn't like it, try purchasing chocolate syrup. There may be sugar in the syrup, but far less than soda pop and the kids will be building healthy bones at the same time.

- Don't succumb to the super-sized drinks. Or, better yet, get milk or juice. On occasion, use club soda, or sparkling water mixed half and half with 100 per cent juice. It's really refreshing.

- Have kids carry a personal water bottle to school, or sports or when traveling.

- If having soda pop, ask for lots of ice in your drink. You get less drink, fewer calories and more water.

Understanding The Media and Celebrity Eating

Studies show that our average families are lucky if they are spending **20 minutes** of quality time together, **PER WEEK** and we, on average, watch more than **2 hours** of TV **PER DAY**!!! Now when we grabbed that statistic, we specifically wanted to know what children were doing. (We used the stats on children from ages 2-11, you can only imagine how much worse they get after that.)

I hope by reading the next few paragraphs you will understand why we, as a continent, are either struggling with weight issues or dealing with eating disorders.

On the one hand when we watch T.V. commercials, we see happy, happy, happy perfectly-put-together moms, feeding their happy, happy, happy children processed foods in boxes (or taking them to their favorite drive through…in which case of course everyone is happy, happy, happy!). On the other we have movie stars walking around with unrealistic wafer thin bodies and perfect hair. Isn't that ironic! We have given our children an unrealistic body type to keep up with, while we're telling them that it's not only ok to eat food that's bad for you, you will actually be *happy, happy, happy* and your parents will be too!

> ## As a parent…what can we do?

When your child tells you that some celebrity is on a diet and they want to eat like their idol…

Tell your child that you will be supportive if **and only if**, they can prove to you that they have researched the diet thoroughly and that they can maintain the exact lifestyle with the exact set of circumstances as their celebrity idol. Their activity level must match the food they're eating and they must prove it to you with research from the library. This way, you as a parent won't be seen as a party pooper. It's extremely important that they understand that their lives are not the same…they can only find that out themselves…with your support.

When your child insists on poor choice packaged food because they were convinced by advertisers the food will improve their life in some way…or if they feel ripped off if they're not going to the local take-out joint regularly…

Suggest one-on-one time instead. Let them pick a junk food look alike meal (like home made chicken burgers, pizza, fajitas, or tacos….with veggies and dip.) Spend the time in the kitchen together instead of the time it would take to drive away from your home in a car. Not only will you be improving the health of your child, you will be leaving them a legacy of taking care of themselves in relation to food and nutrition. Not only that…kids feel proud when they cook…they will gradually know how to make a whole lot of meals and will want to make them for their parents…get it parents? Get it?

My Friend Is On A Diet
and She Looks Really Great!

How many times per month do you hear this? Do you know that recently, the two top selling diets contradicted each other? One said you must always combine a carbohydrate with a protein and one said you must never combine a carbohydrate with a protein. Both of these diet books flew off the shelves in the 100s of thousands. Ask yourself two questions: Why, when 100s of thousands of these kinds of books are being sold, is our continent in worse shape than it's ever been? How could two completely contrary pieces of science make a person temporarily lose weight?

The answers are simpler than you may think. Diets simply do not work in the long run. This doesn't apply to everyone, but it certainly applies to the great majority. It doesn't mean the information is bad on, say, carbs, or lowering fats, or combining foods in different ways. It just means we have to act like the intelligent nation we are, sift out the reasonable stuff and turf the rest.

The problem with "The Diet" is it doesn't encompass a variety of different things, including our very busy lifestyles. "The Diet" also implies we have no responsibilities, no children, no jobs to work around, no partners who have different needs, likes and dislikes. And, worst of all, it requires that we have an abundance of time and money, which 85% of the population doesn't actually have!

So why does "The Diet" work sometimes?

I challenge all of you to go to the bookstore or the library and spend one evening going through all the different diet books. Read between the lines; you'll find out that an important component to the success of "The Diet" revolves around a lifestyle change. It usually requires stepping up your fitness, drinking more water and decreasing your alcohol consumption. Well, those are always good ideas; if we did all three, don't you think this would be a huge factor in the way we look and feel?

I had two "after the fact" conversations recently; let me share the gist of them. The first person was on a restricted dairy diet (she was under the age of 25, ouch!!!). The second was on a diet developed by a doctor to lower your carb intake. I would like to point out that, like many diets, each of these diets is simply on a popularity schedule; in other words, it didn't succeed 20 odd years ago when it was introduced to the North American population, but, we're told, it's sure to work now!

We'll start with the dairy one. This beautiful young girl, even though she wasn't on the diet any more, was adamant that we didn't need calcium. She explained, "many cultures that don't have dairy at all have no signs of osteoporosis." I asked her, "Why did you go off the diet then?"
She explained, "I love dairy. I love cheese and yogurt. The hardest thing I found was that I often have a glass of milk with or around a meal. My job requires me to eat out a lot and the choices for beverages are so limited (either soda pop or juice)."

I showed her a chart which indicates the absorption rate of calcium through different foods (see chart in "Don't pee your bones down the drain."). Then I showed her what Doctors Brett and Lambros had written on calcium and asked her to compare our culture with another culture that doesn't eat dairy. The other culture has virtually no processed foods, take-out or soda pop. And as the doctors wrote, age 13-16 is the really vital age for bone-building.

Then I asked her, "What was your favorite and least favorite part of that diet?" Her favorite part was that she lost weight. Her least favorite was that she gained it all back in short order. She also hated the fact that she constantly craved dairy products and felt deprived through the process. I then asked her, "Was there anything that spoke to you in a good way, while on the diet?" She mentioned that she realized the cramps she used to get were related to overindulging on cheese.

The second person had almost the identical experience, but with carbs. The answer he had when I asked what he liked and disliked the most was the same. He loved that he lost the weight. He hated that he gained it all back. The part that spoke to him was that he had to cut down on his sugar, and he ended up liking hot drinks such as coffee and tea without sugar in them.

I find this over and over again. People end up discouraged after attempting a diet, but they also walk away with something that makes sense to them.

So again, here's the deal: for any of you trying to lose weight, including kids...

- Try eating everything, in smaller portions, more regularly.
- Take away 1/4 of the thing you love that you know you eat too much of.
- Start walking to places more often.
- Pick water over soda drinks at least half the time.

You will be amazed over the long haul what a difference this will make on both your mind and your waistline. The good news is that it's likely to stay that way, because you are developing good—and sustainable—habits!

Those Special Teens and Their Issues

I would like to start by saying, of all the concerns I hear from parents and families across our great continent, the following has got to be the issue that concerns me the most.

I have spoken to so many people who say, "Yeah, I went to my high school reunion and it was a bit shocking. Ten years later…the person who was beautiful or handsome and slim as a rail had ballooned out. Then there was the so-so looking person of average size in high school, who was always active… they now look amazing!"

Teens: You may be living for the day but while you're living for the day, keep in mind that what you do in these teen years will affect the quality of your life as an adult. Habits you form up to age 20 set you up for how you will feel for the majority of your adult life.

Parents, if you hear nothing else hear this: If you nurture your child up to the teenage years with food and then leave nutrition all up to them, you're making a huge parenting mistake.

For some reason, when kids hit adolescence, many parents seem to abdicate their responsibility for making sure healthy meals are on the table. Studies show that, with our busy lives, many families no longer cook or eat together. So those nurturing aspects of food preparation and eating are lost, unless we decide to wrestle them back under our own control as parents.

If you follow the Eating Forward™ steps outlined on page 11-12 in this book, your kids will be taking more and more responsibility in the kitchen - and enjoying it. Then, as they branch out on their own, they'll have the skills to feed themselves in a healthy way. It will keep them away from the yo-yo dieting which can affect their metabolisms so badly that they set themselves up for the ballooning I spoke of above.

Obsessing About Thinness

Another concern I have is the huge overemphasis on thinness in our culture. An obsession for an ideal body type is seen in countless magazines, television shows and on billboards. By using this as the standard, even the average person looks overweight. Not only is obesity on the rise, but so are the eating disorders, anorexia nervosa and bulimia. They don't just happen in teenage girls any more, but are increasingly appearing in younger children including boys, regardless of economic status. Fear of fatness, restrained eating, and binge eating have been found to be common among girls by the age of 10!! While these disorders are a specialized issue beyond the scope of this book, we have included a table of warning signs.

Parents shouldn't be talking about diets with or in front of their children! Parents send strong messages to their children when they constantly complain about their bodies, discuss diets, and obsess over the fat, calorie, and sugar content of every food. Parents have a powerful influence on their children's self-esteem and body image. It has been shown that self-esteem scores of kids ages 9-11 were lower when they thought their parents were dissatisfied with their own bodies.

Warning signs of a serious eating disorder:

- Watch out for young children who obsess about fat in the food they are eating.

- Watch out for children who may be over-exercising and worrying about the number of calories they are burning during physical activity.

- Be alert when a child is too "busy" to eat meals, is extremely picky or disappears into the bathroom after every meal (they could be deliberately vomiting).

- Mood changes are a red flag, such as angry outbursts, isolation from friends, or withdrawn behavior. Watch for drug abuse and depression.

- In girls who have reached puberty, there may be infrequent or absent periods, or physical signs like weight loss, dry skin, hair loss, rashes, and itching (due to lack of protein or vitamins).

Getting Enough Iron

There's a link between iron deficiency and struggling in school. A study on teenage girls found that the more deficient the iron level, the lower the score on a mathematics achievement test. The onset of menstruation in girls around age 12 has been linked to a drop in math achievement. Monthly blood losses place some girls and women at risk for iron-deficiency anemia. Since iron is a component of hemoglobin which carries oxygen in red blood cells, iron shortage can result in fatigue, pale skin, lack of concentration and apathy.

Some Sources of Iron

Lean meat, fish and poultry contain iron that is easily absorbed by the body. Vegetable sources of iron are found in soybeans, lima beans, almonds, raisins, spinach, dried apricots, peas, potatoes and fortified cereals. But this iron is much harder for the body to absorb. To get the most iron from these sources, foods containing Vitamin C such as citrus, broccoli, kiwi, strawberries, or peppers help the absorption. That's why we often serve wedges of oranges with our spinach salad!!

Sandi's Tips

- Be aware as a parent that if your family is constantly dieting, you actually increase the chances of iron deficiencies, weight gain and eating disorders.

- If you suspect your child has an eating disorder, show them through the resources that are available through your local dieticians that starving yourself can actually lead you to weight gain, not weight loss...and get help right away.

Yikes! My Kid is a Vegetarian

Oh boy, do I hear a lot about this one. The question of the day is....Is it okay? Will they be healthy? Will they get all the right nutrients like calcium and many others? Well, if you are asking these questions as a parent, I congratulate you! Many kids and adults decide to adopt a particular way of eating without really knowing the facts ahead of time.

As I tour the continent, I often cook at signings, conferences or events. If the dish happens to have meat in it, I will get at least two or three teens saying, "Oh darn, I can't have that, I'm a vegetarian." This, of course, opens up great conversations. I ask, "What sort of vegetables do you eat?" The answer often is, "Well, I don't really like vegetables." Then I ask, "Are you getting your beans and lentils and legumes and are you eating dark leafy greens at least, like spinach?" This is usually followed by the yuuuuuck squealing sound, followed by, "Well, I don't really like those things." Then I ask, "What are you eating?" Aaaaand, here's the answer: they're eating a ton of pasta, a ton of bread and a ton of cheese. They are not vegetarians, they are simply non-meat eaters. So let's not get confused as to what a vegetarian diet is.

First let's look at the different types of vegetarian eating:

Vegans:
-will only eat foods that are of plant origin like vegetables, fruits, grains, seeds and nuts

Lacto-Vegetarian:
-will include dairy with the plant origin foods

Lacto-Ovo-Vegetarians:
-will also include eggs with the dairy and plant origin foods

Semi-Vegetarian:
-will often have fish and sometimes chicken as well as eggs, dairy and plant origin foods

---

Challenge yourself or your child to ask three important questions before making a huge life-changing decision, such as changing your diet completely!

1. Do I have the time to research this type of eating thoroughly, so that I know how to eat in this way without starving my body of important nutrients?

2. Do I have the support from my family and the self discipline to stick to it?

3. Do I have the financial resources to purchase vitamins to replace the foods I just may not like and am not interested in trying?

   If you can honestly answer "Yes" to these very important questions, great! If you can't, it doesn't mean that vegetarian eating (or others) is out of the picture, it simply means that you have to treat your body like a temple and give it the time it takes to work into a new way of eating.

**How come the movie star vegetarian, whom my child is trying to be like,
is thin and my vegetarian child is gaining weight?**

This is a very common question I am asked by parents and, sure enough, this is a growing problem. In short order, listen up kids; your movie star idols have trainers and coaches and diet advisers. They are making a choice and they are going to get the right information and, more than likely, are taking on the task in a very intelligent way (vegetarian eating can be a very healthy choice if done properly). Parents, I repeat, make sure you and your child have done the research. If they have and they are following a proper vegetarian diet, it will be more like the celebrity's diet. You can bet that the celebrity is not just loading up on bread and pasta.

But how do I feed a vegetarian in the family when the rest of us aren't?

First, refer to the calcium chart on page 28. Show the child the absorption rate of calcium through dairy versus other sources. As a parent, insist that if your child (under the age of 25) expects your support in their efforts to become a vegetarian, they must have the required calcium to build bone density in those critical years. As the child proves that their intake of calcium is sufficient through leafy green vegetables, tofu, soy milk, etc., then you can slowly wean them off dairy and meat and be perfectly comfortable with that one issue. (I bring that up because often teens who claim to be vegetarian cut out milk, but drink a lot of juice and soda pop and this is just baaaaad news! You stop building bone by around age 25, but the really critical ages are the teenage years. So, according to life expectancy, you have less than 1/3 of your life to build bone for the longest part of your life!)

Second, your teens must prove to you that they have gone to the library, dug up the research on what it takes to be a healthy vegetarian, and are willing to do all of the things I mentioned earlier.

How to make dinner a family affair:

Step 1.

I am known as a lover of three-component meals. I suggest you do this as much as possible. (Serve some type of grain or potato, some type of vegetable and some type of protein). I have heard from thousands of families who say this one approach has changed the family dynamics of dinner in a big way. When you serve three-component meals, it takes a lot of stress off the parent or meal maker. Chances are the family member will like two of the three components and therefore will not go away hungry. So the cook doesn't have to feel guilty that their child is hungry, because they're not. It also opens the door for what we call the "One Bite Rule." When there is a family member who is vegetarian, it doesn't alter the entire meal. You may need to have few things handy to add to the components they will eat, like nut mixtures. See the chart on the following page for what you can add to a regular meal if your child is vegetarian.

Step 2.

I also believe the family must get involved in choosing the meals for the Eat Sheet™. When a vegetarian child gets to choose a meal in the week, it makes everyone in the family a little more open to the different likes, dislikes and needs of each family member. This can only be a good thing. These two first steps apply to non-vegetarian families too, and make coping with meals a whole lot easier.

Yikes! My Kid is a Vegetarian (cont.)

Step 3.

Let the child know that because they decide to turn vegetarian, it can't all be up to you, the parent, to make changes in the home with meal preparation or costs. I have a semi-vegetarian at home. He must assist me in making his two favorites, spanakopita (spinach pie) and spinach balls, for the freezer. When the rest of the family is having red meat, these are already cooked and he is in charge of pulling them out and defrosting them to be his replacement.

Don't put a vegetarian child down; help them do the research.

If you have required that a child dig up the information they'll need to keep their body healthy through a vegetarian choice, you need to make sure you're not talking off the top of your hat either. Don't put them down. Look at their research. If it all adds up and the child is willing to share the information with you, just listen up and thank the Heavens above that they are taking such an interest in their own body. As an added bonus, you are bound to learn a few things that you will find helpful to complement your own non-vegetarian eating!

Ideas for Dinners

For a pasta dish

- Divide the sauce. Brown tofu in a separate pan and then add a portion of the sauce you were going to use for the meat dish.

For a meal which includes a salad

- Have nut and raisin mixtures available to add iron and protein.

Look for the celery huggers

- The introduction page to each week's meals explains how to substitute ingredients to create a vegetarian meal.

On dark leafy green salads, add a citrus fruit

- The vitamin C helps the iron be absorbed.
- Crunchy soy nuts are fabulous on salads.

Picky Eaters

Picky eaters—I've been there and it's overwhelming! I honestly believe picky eaters are a result of a parent trying to overcompensate for some of the behaviors of the last generations (like forcing a child to clean their plate). Or we feel guilty for not being home all the time and therefore want the precious time we have with our children to be as happy as possible. Both of these are really a sign of how much we love our children, but we have to understand the consequence of giving that control to the kids. If we allow our children to dictate what they eat, we are giving them reign over one of the most important health decisions of their lives.

For me, as my demands increased at work, this cycle continued. I would come home, my children didn't like what I made, I would resort to a box (chicken fingers, etc.). And before I knew it, they had the impression that dinner came in a box. It wasn't until a child of mine grossed right out when I decided to make home made chicken fingers, that I realized how bad the problem was. The first thing that happened was a squealing squelch of disgust when he realized that chicken fingers came from a "chicken". He kicked and screamed and proclaimed, "I'm not eating them, I want the real kind!" Wherever I go I see teen girls with iron deficiencies because they won't eat meat. It's the new wave of vegetarians. Young girls, who hate vegetables, won't eat beans and lentils because of the texture, but claim to be vegetarians, mostly because they are disgusted with meat.

On the other hand, when my daughter was young, she wouldn't touch anything if it was green. After years of the One Bite Rule, which I'm leading into, she loads her plate with broccoli, saying all along that I'd make her eat it anyway. She'd never admit that she actually likes it now!

Here's what I did to combat my problem with picky eaters. I hear from thousands of families who have put this piece of advice to good use and are so thankful. Give it a try, it's easier than you may think.

The One Bite Rule

Serve only three component meals for the first while. Some type of meat or protein, some type of pasta or rice or potato, and some type of fruit or vegetable. Most kids will like two of the three things. If they are accustomed to getting their way, they will kick up a fuss at first. You, as a parent, must be strong for the sake of their health and the eventual sanity of the home. Repeat to them that this is dinner and that if they don't want to eat it now, it's not a problem, it will be wrapped up for later. I never suggest that a parent force feed a child. If the child really hates something, it's unnecessary to go past the One Bite Rule. Say, "plug your nose, down it with milk, whatever it takes, just one bite. Then eat more of the other two parts that you do like."

Children realize quicker than you may think that you're not giving into high sugar fun snacks later as a reward for their bad behavior. It will become second nature that dinner is dinner, that's it. They don't have to eat it all, but if they don't finish the part they normally like, it's the snack later in the evening. This takes a huge burden off the back of most parents within weeks. They can't believe how it changes the dynamics of dinner in the home, to say nothing of the important health benefits.

Moods, Food and Activity

I spoke at a conference last year about dealing with moods and foods. Afterwards, a dietitian approached me. She said, "Sandi, I'm in charge of a particular district's crisis centers. I just thought you should know that child abuse calls pour in during the dinner hour." She is not suggesting that food in itself is creating problems with child abuse, just that it doesn't help with coping when you are hungry and in chaos.

I've spoken on this topic so many times and I have to say that, even though I know what I'm like when I'm hungry, I had no idea that the problem was so widespread!

Let me tell you what I used to experience many years ago and see if you can relate. I would come home from errands or work. I had mulled over, time and time again during the day, what I was going to have for dinner. I picked up the kids at child care and got home. As I tried to unpack their things, my things, put coats away, the kids would start to beg for my attention. I felt that it was really important to give them my attention because I'd been away all day. We shared information, or a hug, or they showed me their drawings and, all of a sudden, I realized that I really needed to get something going for dinner. As I tried to separate myself from them, they got louder and, it seemed, more demanding. It became increasingly harder to get dinner ready; I started showing my frustration.

There are many scenarios that can finish this story: break into the cracker box for a carb high. Feed the kids something, anything, to keep them quiet. Order in. Take out/drive through. Be mad, unbalanced, and off emotionally while dinner is being prepared. Break into an argument with a partner about how overwhelmed you're feeling.

Have you ever been somewhere having a really great time and then, all of a sudden, out of the blue, you feel sad, tired or mad? Often we realize it could be erratic eating. But we've already started the cycle and it's too difficult to turn around. At this point many people will have something sweet, for example. They will take care of the problem while their sugar levels spike, but they'll feel worse when they come crashing down later.

> **The following three questions and their answers literally solve more than you can imagine.**
>
> - How do you feel when the walk you have procrastinated about finally happens?
> - How do you feel when dinner is planned when you walk in the door?
> - How do you feel when you've made healthy eating choices in the day, and actually enjoyed what you were eating?

If you go for a walk, you boost your endorphins. This lowers your stress levels. You also affect your self esteem by following through with a good choice. Science is starting to show that this one change alone can improve your overall well being.

If your dinner is planned ahead of time, you don't think of food all day and you have a sense of peace that your family is being cared for and so are you.

When dinner is planned you will make better food choices about what you eat during the day. You won't have a high fat lunch, knowing you are going to have a high fat dinner!

Family Meals

Why is sitting down together at dinner so darn important? (I love to tell this story and my kids absolutely hate when I tell it…but oops…) If they have the right to put parents through teenagerhood, we get to tell stories!

Every night, with very few exceptions, we sit down to eat dinner together. It wasn't always this way. I had to get past my pre-conceived view of what sitting down to dinner meant. Here was my fantasy--it would be at about 5:00 or 5:30, my children would learn to have impeccable table manners, we would all laugh and share our day's events and then everyone would pitch in to do the dishes because the children would care deeply for their overworked parents. And all would be beautiful. Yeah…well...NO!!! First I had to get past the 5-5:30 thing. If we are going to eat together, dinner is anywhere between 4:30 and 8:00 depending on the sports or activity schedule. Snacks are doled out accordingly. You may get a whole bagel and fruit if we are eating later. Then…

Here's the reality of it all. When the kids were little, Ron and I would celebrate if we could get through one dinner without someone accidentally knocking their glass of milk over (especially if we were in a restaurant). Now that they are all teenagers, we get the pre-dinner talk. They seem to take turns, so of course Ron and I think it's a conspiracy. The person explains why it is that tonight they just can't stay and talk at the dinner table. As soon as dinner is over, they must immediately get to homework (they try that one first because they know they may have a fighting chance). One will inevitably carry on and on, to the usual response from one of us: "That's nice!" The carrier pigeon elect will then grumble, cross their arms and possibly mumble some foreign thing under their breath. I then ask Ron if I look older than I did a few minutes prior and he responds with his very intelligent response, "You are more beautiful than when I first met you." This is the nightly ritual!

So you are puzzled at this moment, wondering…Are you trying to turn me off making this a nightly event, or are you trying to encourage me?

Here's the cool part: everyone does sit down, dinner is served and one person will bring up some topic within minutes. This topic seems to stir the imagination and opinion of all. Ron and I glance over at each other in amazement--we rarely sit in silence and, in fact, very few volunteer to leave the table. We can sit there for an hour sometimes after we eat. All of a sudden, dishes don't matter, laundry doesn't matter, nothing matters. The jabber of them…that's all that matters. We connect! It's that simple.

Families who choose to make dinner time a ritual will also enjoy the benefits of science which has proven over and over again that when there is a sense of connection, a sense of family, you will live a longer, healthier and happier life!

Parents In Charge…or Parents At Large?

This is the question….You arrive home from the doctor's office. The worst nightmare that could ever occur for any parent just did! The doctor has given you some very grim news about the health of your child. It will take a very important medical decision to reverse this health hazard.

Would you leave this decision up to your ten-year-old? Or would *you* make that decision?

The reason for my question is that I believe many of us leave one of the most crucial medical decisions up to our children every day, when we let them dictate the food they eat and the amount of physical activity they get.

I know that must seem like a harsh statement. After all, there are all those legitimate excuses like, "But I'm already overworked as it is"; "I can't do any more"; "It's too stressful to argue with them".

Well, if my first example didn't get you, maybe this one will. We fuss over our little newborn baby. We check out the new formulas for the proper nutrients and what baby foods are available. We take the baby for immunizations. We get so excited when they grow and then, when they're perfectly healthy toddlers, walking and talking…we let them reverse it all with their food choices based on million-dollar advertising campaigns they see on T.V. and everywhere else they turn.

Do you know that a campaign to get your kids to eat 5 to 10 fruits and vegetables per day has a budget of $700,000, compared to the more than a billion dollar marketing budget for just one fast food franchise? Or the $100 million budget for a nationally-advertised soda drink? Which campaign do you think has a fighting chance?

And now let's hear from the docs….

Mission Possible: The Healthy, Energetic Parent

There isn't a tougher job on the planet than being a parent. The authors of this book are all parents of kids in all different age groups, and completely understand the immense challenges this responsibility entails. One thing we all hold true to our hearts is that we really want what's best for our kids. But sometimes we have to step back and ask ourselves, "What really *is* best for our kids?"

We live in an age where keeping up with the Joneses has taken on epic proportions. In our media frenzy/materialistic world, the pressures to obtain the latest video game system, the DVD and big screen TV, the new computer, etc., etc., etc., are tremendous. These items come with a steep price tag, not the least of which is the "time" price tag, where we're working longer hours just to pay for the extras. We're also expected to be super parents, attending not only every one of little Jane and Johnny's soccer games, but their practices, too. We often spend hours driving so our kids can play a 45-90 minute soccer game. This constant pressure leaves us feeling exhausted, both physically and mentally. When the kids are playing video games or watching TV, we often thank God that we finally have a break. There must be a solution to this madness!

We've talked about the crisis in North America where both adults and kids are consuming too many calories and not burning enough off. This is going to lead to dire consequences for our kids in their adult years. But this isn't just about overweight kids or adults. You'd be astonished at the number of thin men and women who can be seen attending a cardiac care program following their heart attacks or by-pass surgery. It's not always about your body size, it's about leading an overall healthy lifestyle.

As a generation of parents, we've let things get out of control and, if the trends don't stop, our kids are going to have major health problems as adults. A few simple actions will go a long way to help reverse these trends:

1. Don't ever feel guilty when you show the will power to resist buying something you know in your heart is not a healthy choice. Kids need to be spoiled sometimes, but not all the time. If you don't cave in, feel proud of yourself. You have just defeated a multi-billion dollar industry/marketing machine whose sole purpose is to brainwash your kids into thinking they really need that free toy that comes with the fast food meal.

2. Parents are in control of how much time kids spend watching TV, playing computer games, surfing the net, etc. Again, let's be reasonable, kids should be allowed to do these things, but in moderation. Physical activity must replace some sedentary behavior. We also know that kids often snack on high-calorie and/or high-fat foods when they watch TV. At the same time, they're being exposed to tons of advertising for unhealthy food choices.

3. Show your kids the way. Limit your own sedentary behaviors. Walk up the stairs, rather than take the elevator. Park in the farthest corner of the mall parking lot and walk to the store. Walk or ride your bike to get the video. Plan family outings around physical activity. Buy kids toys they will be active with, rather than ones they will be inactive with. Don't use the TV as a babysitter all the time. Talk to your kids about healthy lifestyles and why they're so important. Don't go to extremes, but practice moderation. Only make healthy snacks available.

4. Schools play a huge part in our kids' lives, but participation in physical education has declined. Not only that, many schools have soda and candy machines, and high fat, high calorie meals in the cafeteria. French fries, chips and soda are poor substitutes for a healthy lunch. Push schools to offer more physical education and physical activities which can be carried into adulthood (like tennis, yoga, skiing, running, skateboarding, etc.), not just team sports. Schools should follow the leadership of Los Angeles and eliminate pop machines on school property. Ya, baby! Replace them with milk machines! (Chocolate milk is okay!!)

Kids tend to adopt their parents' behaviors and start developing them in childhood. In other words, if you want your kids to adopt healthy lifestyles, you must lead by example.

The Importance of Breakfast

Yeah, yeah, yeah. Here we go again. We hear it from many sources--breakfast is the most important meal of the day, yet we skip it. In fact we hate being told by people it's important, because we can't seem to pull it off. I'm not talking about all of us, I'm not talking about little ones, where Moms and Dads are ensuring they eat; I'm talking about the general population of middle-school-aged kids up through adults. Aaaand…….the excuses: everything from your basic, "I'm not hungry", to "I'm going to puke if you make me eat."

Now before I lose you (because of course you hate the fact that I'm telling you breakfast is important), let me give you some facts that I think you'll find very interesting. Just recently researchers verified that hungry kids are more likely to have behavioral as well as academic problems than children who are properly nourished. Now this doesn't surprise me at all, considering that studies also show that a breakfast which includes a source of complex carbohydrate fuels your brain cells and you actually learn better throughout the morning hours. Interesting enough, researchers also found that children who ate breakfast actually absorbed far more nutrients from other foods they ate throughout the day, than those children who skipped out on breakfast.

Bad habits usually begin in junior high and middle school, when parents begin to shift the breakfast responsibility to the teens. If the teens see the parents skipping their breakfast, a teen views this as adult-like, and in a sense feels "grown-up" if they no longer have to eat if they don't want to.

Teens also skip breakfast in order to control their weight, but what they need to understand is that breakfast eaters actually tend to be leaner, because they are not as likely to snack on higher calorie foods (like donuts) in the late morning.

Speaking of weight: teens, if you aren't eating regularly, you are actually setting yourself up to get exactly what you don't want--weight problems!!! When you eat, especially breakfast, you actually fire up your burners and speed up your metabolism. Your metabolism will gradually slow down as you age, from where it's at in your youth. If you are slowing it right down now, either by dieting or skipping meals, it will slow down even further as you age and you are at a greater risk of having weight problems.

Now let's hear from the doctors….

By the time you wake up in the morning, it may be over 8 hours since you have had anything to eat. Glucose is the main energy source for the brain but, unfortunately, the brain cannot store glucose. It must constantly be replenished. So eating breakfast gives you an immediate source of glucose for your brain.

Most people will feel better and perform better during the day if they eat breakfast. Research shows that children who skip breakfast are inattentive and do not learn as well in school.

There are also long-term health benefits. According to research, people who eat breakfast have higher intakes of some vitamins and minerals, which makes sense, because calcium, Vitamins A, C, B6, riboflavin and folic acid are found in a typical breakfast of cereal, milk and orange juice. Interestingly, people who skip breakfast don't usually make up for the nutrients they missed.

Keep in mind that children can afford to have some higher fat and higher calorie foods, like cheese, eggs and peanut butter, for breakfast.

Did you know that skipping breakfast can actually make you gain weight? Eating in the morning increases your metabolism during the day, helping you burn more calories. Studies also show that people who skip breakfast eat more during the rest of the day and tend to eat most of their calories in the evening when their activity levels are often lower. While you sleep during the night, your metabolism is even slower and you store extra calories as body fat.

Sandi's Tips

I loooove this! The doctors keep confirming, with their knowledge of science, what I know happens in my own family and hear from families across North America. That's why we moms and dads need to keep insisting our kids eat breakfast. Here are ways to make it easier:

This two-minute smoothie recipe will get everybody's system kick-started:
Blend together 3 cups unsweetened orange juice, 1 cup of yogurt, 4 frozen strawberries, one banana (can be over-ripe) and 8 ice cubes (makes 4 servings). This packs in 2 fruits per serving and fires up those burners, aaaaand the yogurt helps boost your immune system.

Here are some more tips:

- Set the alarm ten minutes earlier.

- Assign a smoothie maker each day, parents included.

- The night before, put breakfast cereal boxes on the table with bowls and spoons. (We all know the kid who looks in the cupboard and says there's nothing to eat. If it's put in front of their face, they're more likely to grab it.)

- Have variety available, but don't flip out if they always eat the same thing for breakfast, as long as they are eating.

- Assign a fruit washer/cutter (kids tend to eat fruit when it's washed and cut).

- Leftovers are fine (let them have leftover rice and pastas, casseroles, etc. from the night before, if that's what they like).

- Put out easy sources of protein, like peanut butter, ready-made egg or salmon sandwich filling, cheese, hard boiled eggs, sliced luncheon meats.

Snacks and Lunches Simplified

Every year when the summer holidays come to an end--the rushing, the school shopping, buying supplies--the kids are back to school or we are back to work and there is a sense of happiness and joy to have the familiar routine, until...we think of LUNCHES!!! YUCK! YUCK! YUCK! (How do I really feel about this topic?)

Well, for the record, I hate them. I hate the hour they must be made, whether it's the morning or the night before. YUCK! YUCK! YUCK!

From the tens of thousands of e-mails I get from parents, they are constantly asking me, "When are you going to publish a book with snack and lunch stuff?"

Well, we do have a whole section on this horrible yucky topic in an upcoming book, buuuut, I decided to give you a sneak preview of a few ideas you can use to take away some of the burden of the lunch hour blues!

First, I want you to ask yourself a few things: Are there times when your children say, "There's nothing to do!" or "I'm bored"? I personally love the one where they stare into the overstuffed cupboards and proclaim, "There's nuuuuuthing to eat!" Why not use that time to have them help out with lunch snacks. Well, despite the fact that I hate to even think about lunches, I have come up with some great time-saving, sanity-saving solutions for the cursed lunch disease! (Sorry folks, I still haven't figured out laundry, although I do have some descriptive words for that, too!)

Put a list on the fridge

Have the names of every member of the family at the top with a column underneath their name, top to bottom. Have them list what they like in their lunch (and will actually eat) in their specific column. Make sure they do it in pencil, not in pen. This doesn't have to be done overnight, start slowly. Leave the list up in case they think of something they didn't think of before. Try not to let them include packaged snacks. I have a couple of exceptions—yogurt and fruit leathers that are 100% fruit. Also, drinking boxes of natural fruit juice are great. You are looking to eventually have 16 commonly-liked snacks. What this does is literally save your sanity. Next...

Alternate what you make

Plan snacks on a four-week rotation. Four different types of snacks per week. (The kids only take 2 per day, but they can alternate the following day). This week the snacks are: chocolate chip cookies, nuts and bolts, yogurt and rice krispie squares. Next week, the snacks are puffed wheat squares, ginger cookies, cheese sticks and cinnamon pita crisps...and so on. Try to have a good variety, because there's one thing I do know about most kids and adults. If they have the same thing over and over again, they'll get sick of it, they'll change their minds and just when you think you have the whole thing figured out, they'll change it all around. This creates a lot of stress for the person doing the grocery shopping because it's overwhelming trying to remember who likes what. Next...

Pre-package

If you listen to nothing else on this page, please listen to this--pre-package. When you make the cookies and they are cooled, package most of them in groups of two. Package puffed wheat or other squares individually. Next...

Set up lunch bins

This I must say was one of my more brilliant ideas. It sounds silly, but it really works. Place a large container in the bottom of your cupboard or pantry. Place a smaller bin in your fridge. Anything that enters into those bins is hands off, unless of course it's for lunch making. These are not allowed to be used for after school snacks, because after school snacks don't need to be packaged. Here's a tip--my kids' after school snack is always fruit, first; then, depending on what we're eating and when, they can also have a piece of toast or a small bowl of cereal. After school is a great time to get in the milk, grains or fruit. (If you have teens, we all know that they certainly won't be seen in public eating… gasp…fruit).

Sharing the load

When it dawned on me that I needed to "Share my information" when it came to a dinner recipe, to get some help from people in my home, I realized I wasn't sharing my information with lunch snacks, either. So I dug up all the lunch snack recipes I could. I then either worked side-by-side with someone to make a snack, or I gave them a snack to make which was age appropriate. I would assign kids to pre-wrap cheese and cracker bundles. (Cheese on a plastic sheet first, fold over so it's completely covered, then the crackers--they don't get soggy this way.) I'll often say, "If you make these and package them for me, you are off dishes tonight." Trade-offs relieve stress and the parent ends up looking like a hero. (That is, when it's time for dishes and the child gets to leave!)

Cinnamon Pita Crisps

Pre-heat oven to 350° F. Melt a small amount of butter and brush the top of as many 7 inch-pita shells as you like. Sprinkle with sugar and cinnamon, then slice into triangles. Place on a cookie sheet, cinnamon side up. Bake for 5 minutes. As they cool, they will crisp up.

---

6 Minute Nuts and Bolts

Melt 1/2 cup butter or margarine in a large microwave-safe bowl. Add 2 Tbsp Worcestershire sauce, 1 tsp onion salt, 1 tsp celery salt and 1 tsp garlic powder (I even add a dash of cayenne pepper). Stir well. Add to bowl in this order: 1 cup peanuts, 2 cups corn bran, 3 cups Shreddies, 2 cups Cheerios and a couple of large handfuls of pretzels. Stir to coat. Microwave at high 1 1/2 minutes. Stir. Microwave again 1 1/2 minutes. Stir. Then microwave a final 1 1/2 minutes. Stir and leave to cool. Keep tossing from time-to-time while they are cooling (they do eventually get nice and crunchy).

For more easy lunch and snack recipes,
visit my website at
www.eatingforward.com

Make Ahead While You're Already Cooking!

I'm often asked the question, "How do you feel about freezing meals ahead of time?"

I'm not fond of the idea, at least the way most people mean it. They're usually talking about a parent taking a few hours aside on the weekend or during an evening, to prepare meals for the week.

Some people will adamantly tell me this is the only way to go! They're almost militant about it… which peaks my suspicion further about how stressed they really are. Why would I be against what seems to be such a common sense solution to avoid takeout or boxed foods? Here's why!

Remember what we talked about earlier…Dinner is much bigger than food. It's not just about food. In fact, when people contact me about how my books have touched their lives, they rarely discuss food; they discuss the issues around food. They say things like, "My husband never helped with dinner before. It's just like you said, he didn't know where to start! Once he had a starting point, he actually enjoys it." They say things like, "I did what you said with my teens, I assigned them each a cooking night. They've started to be a part of meal planning now and I feel like I'm leaving them this great legacy of taking care of themselves." Or things like, "I'm finally taking those pounds off because I'm not even worrying about it anymore! Our family is simply Eating Forward™ as you say we should and, as an added bonus, we sit down to eat together much more often now."

Are you hearing what's important to people? It's the way they feel, it's about their relationships, it's about not feeling hurt because they're finally getting some help in the kitchen, it's about feeling better about themselves. How does this all relate to the whole freeze-ahead thing? Well, you tell me. If you have so little time as it is, and you decide to rob YOU and your family of the few precious hours you have on the weekend so that your week is, let's face it, tolerable, then the issues are much deeper than freezing ahead and they may only get worse!

There is one exception to this rule—and that is--if you really love cooking and freezing ahead! You have a routine where every week you come home with groceries and you prep your meals, the music is blaring and you feel great! Then it's a ME time as well as a work ahead time. So go for it!

For the rest of us, here's what I suggest instead. If you really feel overwhelmed and feel you do need to get ahead of the game by freezing, do simple things that take only minutes. We created a survival week (Week Seven) to give you an idea of what we mean. You can freeze your fresh chicken breasts already marinated in a freezer bag and lay the bag flat, so that it's easy to pull them out, one breast at a time. This way, you can speed up a stir fry, or a chicken burger, or a piece of chicken with rice and a veggie. All of a sudden, it's not overwhelming.

This way, your family is eating well and you don't have to worry about scrounging through the fridge. Let's face it, if you're spending hours of what could be free time on the weekend and not taking care of YOU, the family will have scraps alright…and I'm not talking about food! As Tracy Moland writes in her amazing book *Mom Management*, "The airlines tell parents to put their oxygen masks on first for a reason. If you can't breathe, you can't be there to help your children or partner." Here are some simple ideas for making things ahead while not robbing yourself of precious time.

When making a stir fry with peppers or onions, keep on slivering. Pack up the extra peppers in one freezer bag and the onions in another. Press the bag flat before freezing. This way it's easy to pull out what you'll need for future meals. I have these in the side pocket of my freezer. Heaven is having pre-chopped peppers and onions for my spaghetti sauce.

Speaking of spaghetti sauce...I never make a single batch of any pasta sauce! Always double up on the ingredients. Why? Any pasta sauce can easily be converted to lasagna. I make mango chicken lasagna, curried chicken lasagna, Bengal lasagna! Simply follow the Leftover Lasagna instructions (in week 7) using your leftover sauce. If it's a cream sauce base, you'll need to add extra liquid in the form of milk. If it's tomato base, just use water. These lasagnas take 5-10 minutes to prepare after having your pasta sauce dinner. While someone else is doing dishes, you are getting a lasagna into the freezer. Okay, okay, heaven is also having a lasagna in the freezer.

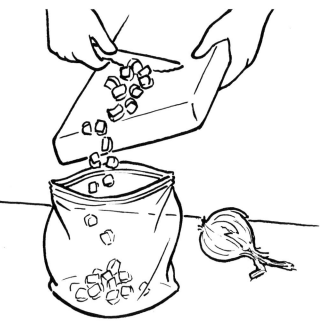

Purchase large packages of chicken breasts when they are on sale. (Use caution when buying the individual frozen variety. They are usually pumped with sodium and a variety of other yucky things. Check the package for ingredients. If it says anything else but chicken, it's not a deal, you're not actually getting your money's worth.) Three chicken breasts are usually close to a pound. Four or five breasts are about 1 1/2 pounds. Take the breasts from the large tray and place them in a freezer bag, lay the bag flat and separate the pieces a little, then seal it. Carefully place it flat in the freezer. Once it's frozen, it's easy to separate the breasts and take out only what you need.

Here are some tips if you are assigning dinners to kids in the week and you work outside the home. If you are worried about a child browning the meat for a casserole, making meatballs for a pasta sauce, or cutting up chicken, you can prep a few things that take only a few minutes, while you're unloading groceries. Cut up 3 chicken breasts in bite size pieces and put them in a small freezer bag, for a stir fry. Brown some meatballs or brown the ground beef for the casserole or sauce. Cool them and freeze them. By doing only part of the meal, you give your family the legacy of independence and cooking skills, and as a parent, you buy yourself some precious time.

Make Your Own

Everyone knows I am a huge fan of using helpers. Helpers are those items that grandma used to make, such as sauces, jams and soups. I believe in our busy lives and working outside the home, it's a good choice to let the food companies make those helpers for you. There are a few, however, that are super easy to make yourself! Here are a few of my favorites.

Homemade Beef, Chicken or Veggie Broth

For **beef**; cut 1 lb of sirloin into chunks and sauté in a little olive oil in a stove-top pot. add to slow cooker.
For **chicken**; cut a deli roaster chicken in half. Add to slow cooker.
For **veggie broth**; simply add the spice and veggies.

Now add; 1 Tbsp basil, 1 Tbsp parsley 1 tsp rosemary, 1 tsp sage, 1/2 tsp curry powder, 1/2 tsp celery salt, 1/4 tsp pepper, pinch chili flakes and 2 bay leaves. (to chicken and veggie also add 1 tsp poultry seasoning)

Wash and cut 2 carrots, 3 ribs celery, 1/2 green pepper, 1 zucchini, 1 onion and 10 mushrooms. Add 1/4 cup white wine and 12 cups water. *You will be shocked how you don't really need the salt if this brews the whole day while you are at work.* Let cool and strain. I like to freeze 10 oz portions in freezer bags.

Homemade Ketchup

Combine two 5 1/2 oz cans tomato paste, 3/4 cup white sugar, 1 cup vinegar, 2/3 cup water, pinch nutmeg, 1/2 tsp paprika, 1/4 tsp celery salt and 1 tsp kosher salt in a medium size stove-top pot. Bring to a boil, then lower heat to a high simmer. Combine 1 Tbsp cornstarch with 3 Tbsp water in a small bowl then whisk into ketchup pot. Continue to simmer at low for 10 minutes, stirring occasionally. Cool and funnel into a bottle.

Homemade Peanut Sate Sauce

Place 3 cups Spanish peanuts, with skins, into food processor. Turn to highest setting and wait until peanuts are completely ground. Drizzle in 1 1/2 cups water, then add 1/2 tsp sambal oelek (ground chili paste), 1 Tbsp sweet soy sauce, 1 1/2 Tbsp lime juice, 1 tsp kosher salt, 1/3 cup demerrera or dark brown sugar and 2 Tbsp dark soy sauce. Funnel into a jar or bottle.

Both the ketchup and sate sauce store beautifully long term in fridge.

Dairy Allergies

I make creamed soups (for my vegan daughter rrrrrgggg) by sautéeing the veggie such as mushrooms, broccoli, asparagus or celery with onion and a salt-free spice. Sprinkle with flour, then add almond or rice milk. These can be cooled and stored in 10 oz servings in freezer containers.

I use tape to label them. When a recipe calls for a soup such as these, just grab yours from the freezer. If the recipe calls for additional milk, make the recipe as you normally would, adding a milk alternative of your choice. If it's an Asian or Indian dish I use light coconut milk.

What The Heck Does A Serving Mean?

You have no idea how many times I'm asked that question. I too was very confused about this when I was struggling to get a handle on my health. You want me to eat how many fruits and vegetables? That's too many. How can I possibly? Here are some thoughts on this whole issue.

I think we're also confused when we hear how many grains we should eat. We think that the number is huuuge. But, in fact, most people don't realize that when they have two slices of toast, they've had two grains. Here's my advice: make the grains count. Find a bread that you like. Experiment. The reason I say this is because Ron tried for years to get the kids hooked on whole wheat bread. He finally resorted to 60% whole wheat which produced a grumble, but at least they ate it. One day he came home with a seven grain bread, left it on the counter (feeling quite safe that no one would devour it), and when he came back, it was all gone. The kids raved about it. It was an easier transition from white to whole wheat after that. They still prefer the grainy one, but it became the stepping stone to whole wheat. (Did you know most multigrain breads are primarily white flour?)

You can also trick them into liking grainy breads by doing things like offering a snack of bread to dip in olive oil and a little balsamic vinegar. Yes, they thought we were freaks at first, but now they just love that treat with a fruit when they come home. (Did you know that the sesame seeds in grainy breads contain calcium?)

About fruits and vegetables: for years I thought I was supposed to get my kids to like green beans. They loved peas, but I thought green beans were better for them. Nope! Peas have tons of iron and are loaded with fiber. I had to learn to be flexible. If I'm cooking a pot of broccoli why not leave a few pieces out for the raw veggie lover? I'm not running a restaurant, but something like that just isn't an extra hassle.

Are the food guides up-to-date? Wow, that's a big one! Remember what they're called--Food Guides. This is because they can only give general guidelines. They don't know how active you are, that's your responsibility. If you want to sit on the couch all night and not even bother with a five minute walk, of course you should adjust things like how much pasta you're eating. We live in a society where everyone else is to blame but us. Come on. Walk, mow the lawn, have a light game of tennis. So I looked like a doorknob the first time I went back and tried a game of tennis after a number of years. I laughed so hard that it felt like I had done sit ups for a day. Who would have thought that laughing was where I was going to get most of my exercise that day?

So when you look over both the American Food Pyramid and the Canadian Food Guide, think about where you fit in to the whole picture. While they're spending mega bucks to give you the most up-to-date knowledge they can muster with the funds they have available, ask yourself what you are doing to fill in the blanks.

Go to **www.healthcanada.gc.ca/foodguide** or **www.mypyramid.gov** for detailed information and great advice on serving sizes for foods in each of the food categories.

What The Heck Does A Serving Mean? (cont.)

Approximate Canadian Serving Sizes

Let's take some of the confusion out of what a serving actually means. It may boost your self esteem by realizing you weren't that far off…or it may put a fire under your butt!

Let's start with the one that freaks most people out:

Veg and Fruit 4-10 servings (This wide range allows for age, sex and activity of person.)

Examples of one serving:

1/2 large banana

1 medium carrot

1 medium apple

1 good sized wedge of melon

1 cup salad (who has a cup of salad!)

If you can visualize a fruit or veggie mis-shaped and stuffed into a tennis ball--that's about a serving.

Here is an example of a typical day:

I take a bag of carrots and veggies to work with me for afternoon snack . . . . . .2 servings

I have a medium fruit when I walk out the door. . . . . .1 serving

I have a salad for lunch . . . . .4 servings

I have broccoli with my dinner . . . . .2 servings

This adds up to 9 servings and I didn't even give it my best effort today.

(Tip: my kids are not allowed to have a snack after school until they have a fruit.)

Grain Products 3-8 servings (This wide range allows for age, sex and activity of person.)

Examples of one serving:

1 cup pasta or rice

1 slice bread

1/2 cup hot cereal

Milk & Alt 2-4 servings (more about guides on page 73)

I really like to make it clear to parents that kids who are not getting enough calcium in their diets are "kind-of" getting osteoporosis now. I say "kind-of" because you don't really get it until later, but you are laying the foundation for the problem during the critical bone-building years.

Examples of one serving:

1 cup milk (I have chocolate syrup on hand for the milk haters…whatever works.)

1 hunk cheese, about the size of two fingers (Cut cheese into long sticks and pre-wrap. It looks more interesting, more like the expensive store-bought variety.)

1 lunch-pack serving yogurt (Try doing things a little differently: freeze the yogurt. Once you get to work or school, it slowly defrosts and tastes like a frozen dessert by the time lunch comes along.)

Make cheese pizza for lunches and individually wrap them once they've cooled. It's easier than making sandwiches and much cooler!!!

Meat & Alt 1-3 servings (more about guides on page 73)

Examples of one serving:

1 chicken drumstick

2 tablespoons of peanut butter

2 eggs

One serving is about the size of your fist. Remember, the size depends on your age, your size, your level of activity and the size of your fist!

Adjusting Nutritional Data
To Your Specific Needs

Before we get to the fun stuff in the upcoming pages, we need to deal with a few details. It's only one page and you don't need to read it like the rest of the book, but can tag it if you want it readily available for easy reference.

- Most of the recipes in The Healthy Family provide 4-6 servings.
- Our test families varied in size. Some families said there was too much food for 4 people, and others thought it was just right.
- If you have 4 adults in your home with very healthy appetites the meal will probably serve 4 (when we write Serves 4-6). Sometimes someone gets a left-over lunch the next day!
- If you have younger children the recipe will probably serve 6 (when we write Serves 4-6).
- When a range is given for the number of servings a meal makes, the higher number is used.
  (i.e. When a meal says 4-6 servings, the nutritional data assumes you are dividing every component of the entire meal into 6 portions. The nutritional data is for one portion of each component. This also applies to the food exchange and food group data.)
  Use the formula below to adjust the nutritional data when we write "Serves 4-6" and for your family it serves 4.

Adjusting Data when a Meal Serves 4 instead of 6

of g fat x 1.5 = # of g fat
i.e. 12 g fat x 1.5 = 18 g fat
(12 g fat per serving for 6 servings) = (18 g fat per serving for 4 servings)

This formula works for all our nutritional data..

Weights and Measures

- Imperial and Metric conversions are approximate only.
- Occasionally we do not provide exact conversions so readers can identify with the can, jar and package sizes produced in their country.
- When more than one unit of measure is provided nutritional data is calculated using the first named.
- When a range is given for a measure, the first given is used to calculate nutritional data.
- When a choice of two ingredients are listed (i.e. chicken or pork), the first is used for nutritional data.
- Ingredients listed as "optional" are not included in nutritional data.
- Fresh garlic (from a jar) is packed in citric acid (not oil).
- Vegetables and fruits are medium size unless otherwise specified.
- Buns are 1 1/2 oz (or 45 g).
- When using cooking spray we assume a 2 second spray.
- **Our meals most often adhere to the following guidelines for the complete dinner.**
  Calories; 350-500 calories/serving; **Fat**; less than 18 g/serving; **Carbohydrates**; 30-70 g/serving; **Protein**; 25-35 g/serving; **Sodium**: less than 1000 mg/serving;
  Calories from fat should not exceed 30% of your total caloric intake each day.

Look Before You Cook

Here is why you look at a recipe ahead of time. How many times have you started to prepare a meal only to find out the meat needed to be marinated for at least an hour? Get the picture? That's why visual triggers such as the Prep Code, crescent moon, slow cooker and BBQ are so helpful. These triggers will help you to match your meal to your schedule.

 Prep Code - see page 74

A **Crescent Moon** above the recipe alerts you to a 5 or 10 minute prep the night before so that the next day is ultra easy. Most of these can be started the same day, in the morning, if your schedule allows.

 A **Slow Cooker** under the clock is a reminder you must prep the night before or the morning of your meal, using a Slow Cooker. The Slow Cooker fills you with wonderful feelings all day knowing that when you get home, your dinner is ready or almost ready.

A **BBQ Grill** under the clock lets you know at least one portion of the meal is grilled. You may need to dig out a grilling pan if you don't own a BBQ grill. Grilling instructions are for a gas or propane grill. If you are using charcoals you will need to adjust.

I also include protein, carb and fruit-veggie symbols to the left of the instructions on each recipe. When you see a symbol - you'll know to shift to a different component of the whole dinner you are making.

 Red circle = some type of **protein**

 Blue square = some type of **carbohydrate**

Green triangle = some type of **fruit or vegetable**

We named this icon **Carrot Top** (I know I'm a little looped in the brain). He helps people who want to eat less meat or are vegetarian. You can find him on the About the Recipes pages with directions telling you what to do to make the meal meatless. Take a look at page 76 and you will see what I mean.

 Also...have fun with the rating page. Kids love getting involved and it makes your life easier when you want to choose meals at a later date. You will see what I mean on page 77.

Notice I never list weekly meals Monday through Friday. That's because I have no idea what your life is like each week. No one can tell you what type of meal you need on any given night except for you. You know who needs to go where, how much time you have or don't have and so on. Maybe you work Tuesday through Saturday.

You Must Own

Cutting Board

Make sure you have a good cutting board that doesn't slip and is easy to pick up. Remember, it's to dump the stuff you're cutting into the pan. I call it my easy food transferer. It's a bonus that it protects my counters.

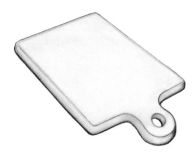

Sharp Knives

We all would love to be able to afford sharp knives of great quality. I slowly purchased mine one at a time and gulped when I paid the price. A temporary fix can be to buy knives that have sharpening holders. If you have dull meat and vegetable knives, it's one more excuse to give up, and we all know, we're looking for any excuse we can get!

Large Microwave-Safe Pot for Rice

Sometimes rice should be cooked on the stove, sometimes in the microwave and sometimes in the oven. It's all a matter of low stress and timing!

Salad Spinner

They are only a few bucks. Watch for a deal, it's an invaluable time saving investment.

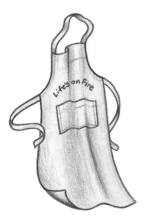

Apron

If you don't have one, buy one....a full length one. There is some strange relationship between changing into your jeans and not making dinner. If you really want work to end, end your work before you change!

Timer

The best investment I ever made for lowering stress at dinner time is an electronic timer. It's for timing you, not the food. When you time yourself during the work week there is a real beginning and more importantly a real end. I say to my family, "I've taken my stuff out and I'm setting the timer." My family knows that means DO NOT DISTURB.

Cutting for Speed

How to cut an onion

trim one end:

cut in half:

peel:

follow the grain to sliver:

cut again to dice:

How to cut a mushroom

trim end, toss out

cut:

lie on flat side:

How to prepare asparagus

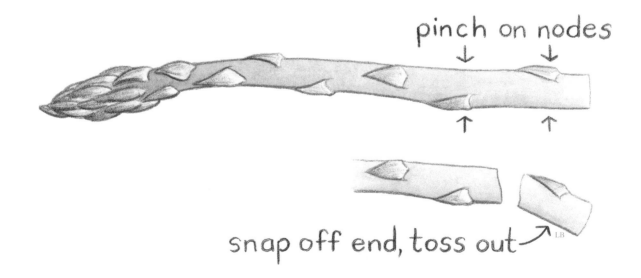

pinch on nodes

snap off end, toss out

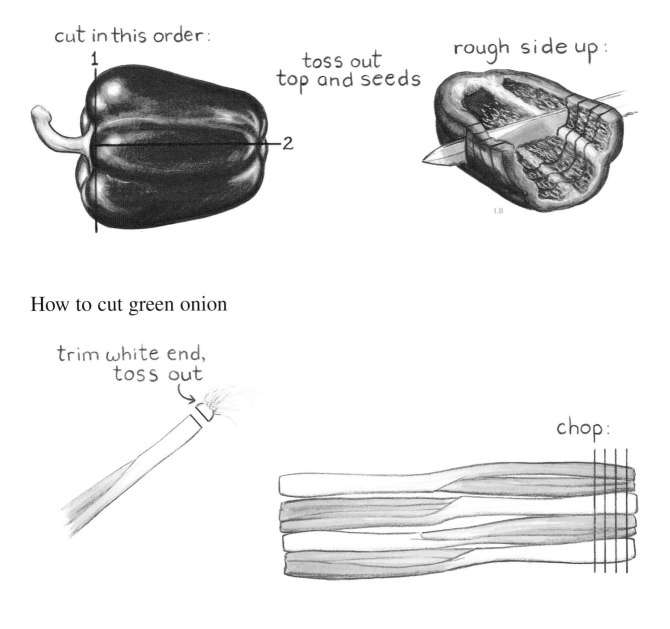

cut in this order:

1

2

toss out
top and seeds

rough side up:

LB

How to cut green onion

trim white end,
toss out

chop:

Chicken breasts are sold in two different ways

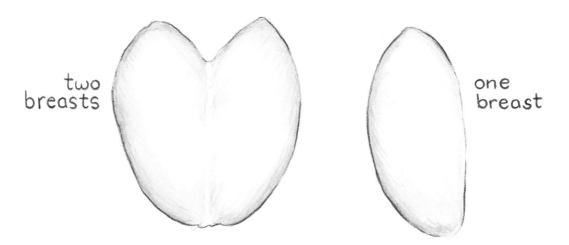

two
breasts

one
breast

Diabetic Food Exchanges and Food Choices

A very large number of people have some form of diabetes, so we feel it is important to include this information as well as the detailed nutritional analysis. Our recipes have very high standards for taste, speed and nutrition. It seems only fair to allow a person with diabetes the luxury of being able to use a regular cookbook with great-tasting meals. They can simply adjust components according to their specific dietary requirements. There is another very important reason for having food exchanges or choices. Some people use food exchanges or choices as a tool to monitor their eating habits for maintaining a healthy weight.

The Canadian Diabetes Association made changes to their meal planning system in 2004. Health Canada has also regulated the Nutrient Value labels found on most food products. Together with changes to medications and methods of managing diabetes, the association has developed the Beyond the Basics resource for meal planning. Beyond the Basics was created to help people eat healthy meals and thus follow a healthy lifestyle to promote optimal diabetes management, based on Canada's Food Guide.

With information about carbohydrates people can keep their intake of carbohydrates consistent. A carbohydrate choice contains 15 grams of available carbohydrate (fiber is subtracted from total carbohydrate). Fruit, milk and starches are included in the carbohydrate choices. Vegetables are considered to be free when consumed in 1/2 cup (125 mL) portions. Visit **www.diabetes.ca** for information and resources from the **Canadian Diabetes Association**'s website.

The American Diabetes Association's Exchange Lists have also been revised recently. They have developed the Diabetes Food Pyramid, grouping foods based on their carbohydrate and protein content in order to keep carbohydrate content consistent. This new list helps one get more variety through a flexible eating plan. Visit **www.diabetes.org** for the exchange list, the pyramid, information, and resources from the **American Diabetes Association**'s website.

Canada's Choices and America's Exchanges are included for each meal in our book.

Equipment List:	Per serving:	
BBQ or broiler pan	Calories	328
BBQ tongs	Fat	7.8 g
Large stove-top pot	Protein	26.5 g
Small stove-top pot	Carbohydrate	39.0 g
Cutting board	Fiber	4.9 g
Colander	Sodium	94 mg
Medium serving bowl		
Sharp veggie knife		
2 stirring spoons	U.S. Food	Cdn. Food
Fork	Exchanges:	Choices:
Measuring cups and spoons	2　　Starch	2 1/2 Carb
Aluminum foil	3　　Meat-lean	3　　Meat/Alt
	1　　Vegetable	

Nutritional data, including food choices and exchanges, are calculated for the entire meal (per serving).

Sodium content is included for the benefit of those monitoring salt intake.

Food Guides

I believe, as I always have, that the Food Guides are right on track. The problem has been the people reading them!

Sooo...both the USDA Food Guide Pyramid and Canada's Food Guide can now be personalized to your needs by going to their websites.

Before, the guides didn't know how much exercise you got. They didn't know anything about you, so it was your responsibility to follow the guides according to your specific information. Now they do the thinking for you. You key in your information and they provide you with a plan customized to your needs. If you cut my plate into three parts, half would be veggies. The other half of the plate would be split between protein and grains. That's how the guide works for me. Why? Because I only manage to exercise three times a week, and the rest of the time I am standing at a kitchen counter or working at a computer. My daughter Paige, on the other hand, played college basketball and now coaches high school basketball while she's finishing her teacher's degree, so she needs a few more grains than I do because she is far more active.

We also have to look at the guide from a financial standpoint. When the kids were little I purchased far more things like pasta and bread because it was inexpensive and I had to make my dollar stretch. But, I was running from morning 'til night and as a sanity break had a brisk walk every morning, so I was able to burn off what I ate. You can't go heavy on bread and sweets if you're sitting at a computer all day, come home, then sit on the couch. If you do that, you'll get fat and you can't blame the guides.

Go to **www.mypyramid.gov** or **www.healthcanada.gc.ca/foodguide** and enjoy their new interactive approach to making your eating life easier to understand.

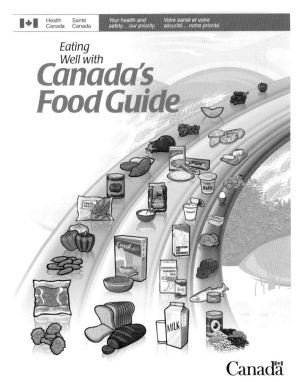

CANADA
healthcanada.gc.ca/foodguide

The Prep Code

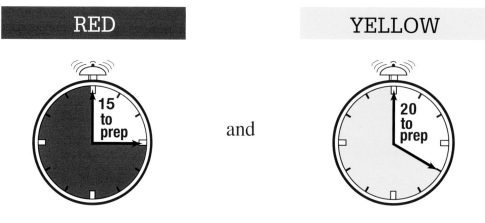

RED	YELLOW
Less Cutting and Chopping	More Cutting and Chopping

Dinner's ready in **30 minutes** or less
...when you need to get your butt out of the house fast.

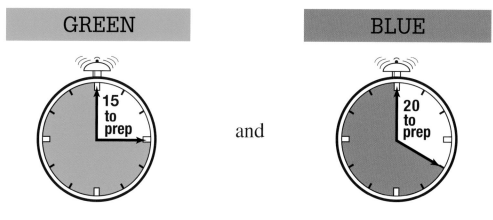

GREEN	BLUE
Less Cutting and Chopping	More Cutting and Chopping

Dinner's ready in **60 minutes** or less
...when you have a small window of opportunity to prep,
but need to rush off somewhere while dinner is cooking,
or you want to relax before you eat.

About the Recipes

Green

YUUUUUMMY!!!!! This is so mouth watering that, despite the fact that it's 5:00 a.m. as I write, my mouth is having a little fit!
Note: there is a lot of liquid and you may feel something is wrong. There is nothing wrong. The beautiful liquid sucks itself up into the chicken and creates this amazing flavor. Our family tends to drizzle the remaining liquid on the potatoes!!! This dish is also great with rice.

Red

I remember thinking how weird flank steak looked in the store and how I was never interested in buying it. Well, if you haven't tried flank steak in a stir-fry, now's the time. Here's the cool part…it usually comes in large packages. Ron and I cut what we need for dinner and then, right after dinner, slice up the rest into packages for the freezer! Vegetarians: Tofu and mixed beans, such as garbanzo and romano, are fabulous in this sauce!

Blue

These are "To die for". Kids, when you are stuffing the manicotti, do it with a small spoon over the pan. This isn't a neatness contest, so don't worry if some of the stuff falls out. Only fill them about 3/4 full because the pasta will soften and surround the meat nicely. Once the sauce goes over top, they will come out looking amazing. Note: Don't forget to spray the pan, add the extra liquid, and close the foil very tightly. Vegetarians: Veggie grind is absolutely fantastic in these!

Yellow

I remember the first time I heard from a friend of mine that these ingredients were great together (tomato soup and applesauce), I thought it sounded disgusting. Take my word for it, it's well worth the try! I haven't met a kid who doesn't love these! Note: Make sure you use extra lean ground beef to keep the fat down. If you're not in a rush, you can bake these in the oven next to the rice for 1 hour, instead of pan frying them.

Red

This is the junk food meal of the week. As you can see by the nutritional data… it's not very junk foodish (but don't tell anyone)! When I get home with my groceries for this week, I immediately make the sauce, throw it in the freezer bag with the chicken, smoosh it to coat and toss it in the freezer. It's done, over, finished! I loooove freebee meals! Vegetarians: Broil a portabella mushroom with onion and pepper slivers on top. Drizzle with olive oil, then sprinkle with pine nuts and Parmesan cheese if you like. Spread the BBQ sauce on the bun and NUMMMY!

Week 1

Green: Crunchy Orange Curried Chicken
with Potatoes and Salad

Our family rating: 9.5
Your family rating: _____

Red: Asian Beef with Snow Peas and Rice

Our family rating: 10
Your family rating: _____

Blue: Easy Turkey Manicotti with Italian Veggies

Our family rating: 8.5
Your family rating: _____

Yellow: Meatballs in Applesauce
with Rice and Broccoli

Our family rating: 8
Your family rating: _____

Red: BBQ Chicken Burgers with Veggies and Dip

Our family rating: 10
Your family rating: _____

Crunchy Orange Curried Chicken with Potatoes and Spinach Salad

Instructions:

Don't change yet! Take out equipment.
1. Preheat **oven** to 350° F.

2. Combine orange juice, brown sugar, honey and mustard in a small bowl. Stir.

Unravel chicken thighs and place in a large lasagna or cake pan. *Squish them together if you need to.* Spoon all the sauce evenly over chicken pieces.
Sprinkle with spices and corn flake crumbs.

Bake in **preheated oven**.
Set timer 50 minutes.

3. Wash potatoes, then add to a different oven-safe pan. Drizzle with olive oil and toss until potatoes are well coated. Sprinkle with spice. Place in **oven** beside chicken.

4. Rinse spinach leaves under cold water in salad spinner and spin dry. Place in salad bowl. Slice orange wedges and toss into greens.

Set aside in **fridge**.

Combine mayonnaise, yogurt and poppy seeds in a small bowl in that order. Stir to blend, using a whisk or a fork, until smooth.
Set aside on table.

...when timer rings for chicken...
Dinner is ready.
This has such an amazing aroma while it's cooking, that by the time you eat you feel like the journey was half the fun.

Ingredients:

Take out ingredients.

1/2 cup orange juice, unsweetened
2 Tbsp brown sugar
2 Tbsp liquid honey
1 Tbsp Dijon mustard

chicken thighs, boneless, skinless
  (1 3/4 lb or 800 g)

2 tsp curry powder
1/4 tsp pepper
1 tsp table blend seasoning, salt-free
1 cup corn flake crumbs
You can buy these already crushed in the coating mix section of your grocery store... or you can crumble them in your hand directly over the chicken in the pan.

20 baby potatoes (or cut up 4 large)
1 Tbsp olive oil, extra-virgin
1 tsp Mrs. Dash Original Seasoning

12 oz or 350 g pre-washed baby spinach
2 oranges

Healthy Poppyseed Dressing
1/4 cup mayonnaise, light
1/4 cup French vanilla yogurt, low-fat
1/4 tsp poppy seeds
You may want to whisk in a tiny bit of 1% milk if you like your dressing a bit runnier.

Oh yes...you may want to add a few croutons to your salad like we do.

Serves 4-6

DINNER IS READY IN 60 MINUTES

Equipment List:

Large lasagna or cake pan
Medium oven-safe pan
2 small mixing bowls
Cutting board
Salad spinner
Salad bowl
Salad tongs
Sharp veggie knife
Stirring spoon
Fork
Measuring cups and spoons

Per serving:

Calories	475
Fat	11.7 g
Protein	33.2 g
Carbohydrate	62.0 g
Fiber	6.5 g
Sodium	390 mg

U.S. Food Exchanges:		Cdn. Food Choices:	
3	Starch	4	Carb
4	Meat-lean	4	Meat/Alt
1	Fruit		
1/2	Fat		

Asian Beef with Snow Peas and Rice

Instructions:

...the night before...
Take out equipment.

1. Combine the following in a medium size mixing bowl in this order: cornstarch, stir in soy sauce, gradually add water, red wine and sugar.

   Slice beef against the grain in strips approx 2" long. Add to marinade bowl as you cut. Toss with a fork until well coated.
   Cover and leave in **fridge** overnight.

   Combine the following in another small bowl or container: cornstarch, blend in oyster sauce, sesame oil, sugar, water, Thai peanut sauce, garlic, and chicken broth.

   Cover and leave in **fridge** overnight.

...when you get home for dinner...

2. Combine rice and water in a large microwave-safe pot or casserole. Cover and **microwave** at high 10 minutes, then medium 10 minutes.

3. Heat oil in a large nonstick **fry pan** or wok at med-high. Add ginger, drained marinated beef and chili flakes.

   Slice green onion and add to pan as you cut.
   Toss until meat browns.
   Add stir-fry sauce and snow peas.

   Toss until sauce thickens slightly and snow peas are tender but crisp.

Ingredients:

Take out ingredients.
Marinade
1 Tbsp cornstarch
1 Tbsp soy sauce, reduced-sodium
2 Tbsp water
1 Tbsp red wine (can be non-alcoholic)
1/2 tsp sugar

1 lb or 450 g flank steak (or sirloin steak)

Stir-fry Sauce
1 tsp cornstarch
2 tsp oyster sauce
1 tsp sesame oil
1/2 tsp sugar
1 Tbsp water
1 Tbsp Thai peanut sauce
  (can be Szechuan or peanut satay)
1 Tbsp prepared garlic (from a jar)
3/4 cup chicken broth, reduced-sodium

1 1/2 cups basmati or white rice
3 cups water

1 tsp sesame oil
1 tsp ginger powder
  (or 2 tsp prepared ginger...from a jar)
marinated beef
  (drain the marinade liquid and discard)
1/2 tsp red crushed chilies (optional)
2 green onions
reserved Stir-fry Sauce
1 1/3 lb or 600 g frozen snow peas
  (or use fresh)

If you like things spicy, increase the hot pepper flakes to 1 tsp from 1/2 tsp.

Serves 4-6

DINNER IS READY IN 25 MINUTES

Equipment List:

...the night before...

Medium mixing bowl
Small mixing bowl
Cutting board
Sharp meat knife
2 stirring spoons
Fork
Can opener
Measuring cups and spoons

...when you get home...

Large nonstick fry pan or wok
Large microwave-safe pot w/lid
Sharp vegetable knife
2 stirring spoons
Measuring spoons

Per serving:

Calories	348
Fat	7.3 g
Protein	23.3 g
Carbohydrate	45.8 g
Fiber	4.5 g
Sodium	212 mg

U.S. Food Exchanges:		Cdn. Food Choices:	
2 1/2	Starch	3	Carb
3	Meat-lean	3	Meat/Alt
1	Vegetable		

Assumes 2/3 marinade discarded.

15
to
prep

W
E
E
K

1

Easy Turkey Manicotti with Italian Veggies

Instructions:

Don't change yet! Take out equipment.

1. Preheat **oven** to 375° F.

   Brown ground turkey in a large nonstick **fry pan** or wok at med-high. Add spice. Once meat is thoroughly cooked, add soup and milk to the pan, in that order.
   Mix well to combine, then **remove from heat**.

   Spray lasagna or cake pan with cooking spray. Tip uncooked manicotti on end and spoon in filling until it's about 3/4 full. *It doesn't matter if the stuff is falling onto the pan and doesn't look so neat...it looks just beautiful once everything is cooked!* When all shells are filled and in pan, spoon cottage cheese over top, then spoon pasta sauce over top.

   Sprinkle on Parmesan and cover tightly with foil shiny side down. Bake in **preheated oven**. Set timer for 50 minutes.

2. Wash and chop celery, pepper and cucumber. Rinse baby carrots.
   Place veggies in a med-size bowl.

   Toss with olive oil, balsamic vinegar and spice.
   Let stand in **fridge**.

3. When timer rings for manicotti, uncover. Grate cheese directly over top.
   Return the pan to oven and set oven to **broil**. Watch it very carefully as it only takes a couple of minutes to bubble up.

Ingredients:

Take out ingredients.

1 lb or 450 g ground turkey
1/2 tsp table blend seasoning, salt-free
1 tsp curry powder
1/4 tsp pepper
1 can cream of mushroom soup
 (10 fl oz or 284 mL)
1/4 soup can 1% milk

cooking spray
8 oz or 250 g manicotti noodles

1 cup 1% cottage cheese (8 oz or 250 g)
1 can tomato pasta sauce
 (24 fl oz or 680 mL)
 I use a spicy blend. Choose a low sodium brand to reduce your sodium intake.

1/4 cup Parmesan cheese, light, grated
aluminum foil

2 celery ribs
1/2 red bell pepper (or 1 small)
1 cucumber (English or field)
1 cup baby carrots

1 Tbsp olive oil, extra-virgin
1 Tbsp balsamic vinegar
1 tsp Italian seasoning

1 cup grated mozzarella cheese, part-skim, shredded

Serves 4-6

DINNER IS READY IN 60 MINUTES

Equipment List:

Large nonstick fry pan or wok
Large lasagna or cake pan
Cutting board
Med-size bowl
Cheese grater
Can opener
Aluminum foil
Sharp veggie knife
2 large serving spoons
Large stirring spoon
Measuring cups and spoons

Per serving:

Calories	483
Fat	15.4 g
Protein	32.2 g
Carbohydrate	52.1 g
Fiber	5.4 g
Sodium	959 mg

U.S. Food Exchanges:		Cdn. Food Choices:	
2	Starch	3	Carb
3 1/2	Meat-lean	4 1/2	Meat/Alt
2	Vegetable	1/2	Fat
1	Fat		
1/2	Milk-fat free		

20 to prep

Meatballs in Applesauce
with Rice and Broccoli

Instructions:

Don't change yet! Take out equipment.

1. Combine rice and water in a large microwave-safe pot with lid. **Microwave** at high 10 minutes, then medium 10 minutes.

2. Combine beef, garlic powder, onion powder and pepper in a mixing bowl.

   Form into 1" meatballs and place in large nonstick **fry pan** on medium heat, adding to pan as you form each meatball.
   Start by placing the meatballs on the outside of pan moving toward the center.
   Chop onion, then add to pan.

   In the uncleaned bowl, combine applesauce, tomato soup, honey and chili paste.

   Once meatballs have browned, pour sauce over top. Stir to coat.
   Once sauce starts to boil, **reduce heat** to a high simmer.

3. Rinse broccoli in colander or steamer basket. Place a small amount of water in the bottom of a **stove-top** pot and bring to a full boil with the broccoli in the basket above. Cover and set timer for 3 minutes. ...or microwave at high for 3 minutes.
   Add butter if you must.

Ingredients:

Take out ingredients.

1 1/2 cups basmati or white rice
3 cups water

1 1/2 lbs or 675 g ground beef, extra-lean
1 tsp garlic powder
1/2 tsp onion powder (can be onion salt)
1/4 tsp pepper

1/2 cup chopped onion (fresh or frozen)

1/2 cup applesauce, unsweetened
1 can tomato soup (10 fl oz or 284 mL)
1 Tbsp liquid honey
1/2 tsp Sambal Oelek (crushed chili paste)
 (add more if you like it hot)

1 lb or 450 g broccoli florets
water

butter (optional)

Serves 4-6

DINNER IS READY IN 30 MINUTES

Equipment List:

Stove-top pot w/steamer basket
Large nonstick fry pan
Large microwave-safe pot w/lid
Large mixing bowl
Colander
Cutting board
Sharp veggie knife
Stirring spoon
Can opener
Measuring cups and spoons

Per serving:

Calories	433
Fat	12.8 g
Protein	26.9 g
Carbohydrate	52.9 g
Fiber	2.2 g
Sodium	368 mg

U.S. Food Exchanges:		Cdn. Food Choices:	
2 1/2	Starch	3	Carb
3	Meat-lean	4	Meat/Alt
1	Fruit	1/2	Other
1	Fat		

20 to prep

BBQ Chicken Burgers with Veggies & Dip

Instructions:

Don't change yet! Take out equipment.

1. Place chicken breasts into a large resealable freezer bag. *Have the bag sitting upright with the mouth of the bag open.*
   Add the following ingredients into the bag with the chicken breasts: ketchup, brown sugar, salsa and Worcestershire sauce.

   Close the bag tightly and smoosh everything together. Set aside in **fridge**.

2. Rinse baby carrots, celery and pepper. Cut celery into sticks and sliver pepper.

   Rinse broccoli and cut into bite size pieces.

   Set aside in **fridge** on a serving plate.

   Combine mayonnaise, sour cream and seasoning into a small serving bowl.
   Mix well and set aside in **fridge**.

3. Slice buns and get fixings ready.
   (e.g. mayonnaise, lettuce, tomato, things you would normally enjoy on a chicken burger)

4. Broil chicken in oven on **broil** or **grill** on the BBQ.
   Turn once, until cooked throughout.

Ingredients:

Take out ingredients.

**4 chicken breasts, boneless, skinless
 (1 1/2 lbs or 675 g)
1 large resealable freezer bag**

**1/2 cup ketchup
2 Tbsp brown sugar
2Tbsp cup salsa
1 tsp Worcestershire sauce**

**1 lb or 454 g baby carrots
2 celery ribs
1/2 red or yellow bell pepper** (or 1 small)
1/2 lb or 225 g broccoli florets
Here's a tip for buying red and yellow peppers, which can be quite expensive. Pick several up in your hand…purchase the one that weighs the least. Peppers can be huge and very light, or small and very heavy. You're not using the inside anyway and this way you can actually afford them.

Low-Fat Veggie Dip
**1/4 cup mayonnaise, light
1/4 cup sour cream, no-fat
1/2 tsp garlic & herb seasoning, salt-free**

**6-8 hamburger buns, whole wheat
fixings of your choice** (optional)

Serves 4-6

DINNER IS READY IN 25 MINUTES

Equipment List:

Broiler pan or BBQ grill
Colander
Cutting board
Small serving bowl
Serving plate
Sharp veggie knife
Sharp bread knife
Spreading knife
Stirring spoon
Measuring cups and spoons
Large resealable freezer bag

Per serving:

Calories	364
Fat	7.3 g
Protein	32.7 g
Carbohydrate	43.9 g
Fiber	5.3 g
Sodium	710 mg

U.S. Food Exchanges:		Cdn. Food Choices:	
2	Starch	2	Carb
4	Meat-lean	4	Meat/Alt
1/2	Fruit	1/2	Other
1	Vegetable		

About the Recipes

Red

Ten, do you see that, ten?! That is the rating my family gives this recipe. It may sound like a very odd combination of foods, but believe me, this dish is truly a taste experience! If you are vegetarian, you can fry up some firm tofu and finish it off with some almonds. WOW!!!

Blue

I love to experiment with different flavors. Tossing things like dried cranberries into recipes can add such an unusual touch to both flavor and appearance. This is such an easy recipe to prepare. A great entertaining dish, too. It will look like you fussed for hours!

Yellow

This is a "feel good" meal. It's one of those meals that makes you feel like you've had a hug! If you or your kids aren't crazy about salmon, you can easily replace it with canned chicken or tuna. If you like salmon, however, it's a really healthy choice to leave it just the way it is. If you are vegetarian, you can toss in crumbled firm tofu.

Green

Nummy, nummy, nummy, nummy, nummy, nummy, nummy!!!!!
This is such a great "night before preparation" because there is almost nothing to do and you can stick the frozen solid roast into the slow cooker. I call this my life saver meal. I always feel like I've served my family a home cooked meal...and I've done almost nothing!!!

Yellow

This is the junk food meal of the week. When I first created this very weird pizza, only Ron and I really liked it. We have the One Bite Rule in our family, however, so the kids had to have a bite every time we made it. It was never a hassle to make two pizzas, one for them that was more standard and the Thai pizza for us. In fact, we preferred they didn't like it--more for Ron and I!! Now the kids won't have anything-but. It's one of those meals that just keeps growing on you. Give it a try. Vegetarians: Slivered almonds and roasted vegetables on this are absolutely amazing!!!!

Week 2

Red: Hot Beef and Pasta on Caesar Salad

Our family rating: 10
Your family rating: _____

Blue: Maple Cranberry Chicken Breasts
with Rice and Broccoli

Our family rating: 9
Your family rating: _____

Yellow: Curried Salmon and Egg Noodle Bake
with Peas

Our family rating: 8 and growing
Your family rating: _____

Green: Savory Pot Roast with Harvest Veggies

Our family rating: 10
Your family rating: _____

Yellow: Thai Chicken Pizza with Veggie Toss

Our family rating: 10
Your family rating: _____

Hot Beef and Pasta on Caesar Salad

Instructions:

Don't change yet! Take out equipment.

1. Fill a large **stove-top** pot with water and bring to a boil.
   …meanwhile…

2. Heat oil in a large nonstick **fry pan** or wok at med-high. Cut beef into thin strips, against the grain, and gradually add to pan as you cut. Stir.

3. Place pasta in boiling water and set timer according to package directions, approx 10 minutes.

4. Sliver onion, then rinse and slice mushrooms adding to meat pan as you cut.
   Add garlic, ginger, and chili flakes.

   Add teriyaki sauce and vegetable juice to pan and stir.

   Sliver red and yellow peppers. Rinse and cut broccoli into bite size pieces. Add to pan.

   …when timer rings for pasta…

5. Rinse pasta in colander and let drain.

6. Add pasta to meat pan and stir.

   Tear lettuce in bite size pieces directly into salad spinner. Rinse and spin dry.
   Arrange lettuce on serving plates.
   Blend dressing with mayonnaise in a coffee mug and drizzle evenly over lettuce.
   You may want to whisk in a tiny bit of 1% milk if you like your dressing a bit runnier.

   Evenly distribute the pasta stir-fry on top of lettuce.

Ingredients:

Take out ingredients.

water

1 tsp sesame oil
1 lb or 450 g flank steak (or chicken)

2 cups spiral pasta, whole wheat

1/2 onion
5 mushrooms
1 tsp prepared garlic (from a jar)
1/2 tsp ginger powder
1/2 tsp hot chili flakes (optional)

1/2 cup teriyaki sauce, reduced-sodium
1/4 cup vegetable juice
   You can substitute clamato juice for vegetable juice. We like the spicy variety.
1/2 red bell pepper
1/2 yellow bell pepper
1/2 lb or 225 g broccoli florets

1 head leaf lettuce

Easy Caesar Dressing (Lower Fat)
3 Tbsp gourmet Caesar salad dressing, light
mixed with,
3 Tbsp mayonnaise, light
   Mega flavor but lower fat.
   Grating a little Parmesan or cheddar on top is a really nice touch for appearance and taste.

Serves 4-6

DINNER IS READY IN 25 MINUTES

Equipment List:

Large stove-top pot w/lid
Large nonstick fry pan or wok
2 cutting boards
Colander
Salad spinner
Salad tongs
Sharp meat knife
Sharp veggie knife
Large stirring spoon
Coffee mug
Measuring cups and spoons
Serving plates

Per serving:

Calories	341
Fat	10.7 g
Protein	26.2 g
Carbohydrate	38.5 g
Fiber	4.5 g
Sodium	654 mg

U.S. Food Exchanges:		Cdn. Food Choices:	
2	Starch	2	Carb
3	Meat-lean	3 1/2	Meat/Alt
1	Vegetable	1/3	Other
1/2	Fat		

15 to prep

W E E K 2

Maple Cranberry Chicken Breasts with Rice and Broccoli

Instructions:

Don't change yet! Take out equipment.

1. Melt butter in a nonstick **fry pan** on medium heat. Add garlic.
   Place flour, salt, pepper and rosemary in a bowl or plastic bag.

   Coat the chicken pieces in flour mixture and brown in pan on both sides.
   Cut green onion and slice mushrooms.
   Add to pan as you cut.
   …meanwhile…
   Mix together maple syrup, vinegar and water.
   Pour over chicken once chicken is browned.
   Sprinkle cranberries around chicken pieces.
   Reduce heat to a high simmer.

   Set timer for 20 minutes. *Check the chicken frequently to make sure the liquid isn't evaporating too much. Add a little water at a time if it is. You want it a little saucy.*

2. Combine rice and water in a large microwave-safe pot. Cover and let stand in microwave until timer rings for chicken.
   …when timer rings for chicken…
   Reduce heat for chicken to a low simmer.
   Microwave rice at high 10 minutes, then medium 10 minutes.
   …when timer rings for rice…
   Chicken and rice are ready.

   …meanwhile…
3. Rinse broccoli in colander or steamer basket.
   Place a small amount of water in the bottom of a **stove-top** pot and bring to a full boil with the broccoli in the basket above. Cover and set timer for 3 minutes. …or microwave at high for 3 minutes.
   Toss with spice and butter if you wish.

Ingredients:

Take out ingredients.

2 tsp butter
2 tsp prepared garlic (from a jar)
1/4 cup flour
1/8 tsp salt
1/8 tsp pepper
1/8 tsp rosemary leaves

**4 chicken breasts, boneless skinless
  (1 1/2 lbs or 675 g)**
3 green onions
10 mushrooms

1/2 cup maple syrup
2 Tbsp apple cider vinegar
2 Tbsp water
1/4 cup dried cranberries, unsweetened

1 1/4 cups basmati or white rice
3 cups water

1 lb or 450 g broccoli florets
water

**1/2 tsp table blend seasoning, salt-free
butter** (optional)

Serves 4-6

DINNER IS READY IN 60 MINUTES

Equipment List:

Large nonstick fry pan
Large microwave-safe pot w/lid
Stove-top pot w/steamer basket
Colander
Cutting board
Small mixing bowl
Mixing bowl or plastic bag
Sharp veggie knife
Measuring cups and spoons

Per serving:

Calories	475
Fat	4.0 g
Protein	32.5 g
Carbohydrate	77.5 g
Fiber	3.2 g
Sodium	157 mg

U.S. Food Exchanges:		Cdn. Food Choices:	
4	Starch	4	Carb
3 1/2	Meat-lean	4	Meat/Alt
1	Other Carb	1	Other

20 to prep

WEEK 2

Curried Salmon and Egg Noodle Bake with Peas

Instructions:	Ingredients:
Don't change yet! Take out equipment.	Take out ingredients.

1. Preheat **oven** to 375° F.

2. Fill a large **stove-top** pot with water and bring to a boil.

   water

   <u>Milk Mixture</u>
   2 Tbsp butter or margarine
   2 Tbsp flour

3. Melt butter in a med size **stove-top** pot at med heat. Once butter is melted, **remove from heat** and blend in flour with a whisk or fork. Whisk in milk very gradually. **Return to heat**. Add spices and stir constantly at med heat until slightly thickened. **Remove from heat**.

   2 1/2 cups 1% milk
   1 tsp Mrs. Dash Original Seasoning
   1 tsp curry powder
   1/4 tsp fresh ground pepper

4. Place noodles in boiling water. Set timer for 5 minutes – you just want them softened.

   3/4 lb or 340 g broad egg noodles
   No Yolks variety are my favorite, or use whole wheat noodles to increase your fiber.

5. Rinse noodles in colander, return to pot and add milk mixture to noodles. Crumble salmon into pot. Grate cheese and add to pot. Stir. *Drain salmon first, if using canned.*

   3/4 cup cooked salmon, boneless, skinless
   (use canned or fresh - we use pink salmon)
   3/4 cup cheddar cheese, light, shredded

   Spray a large lasagna or cake pan with cooking spray and toss in salmon mixture. Cover tightly with foil and place in **preheated oven**. Set timer for 20 minutes.

   cooking spray

   aluminum foil

6. Rinse peas in colander or steamer basket. Place a small amount of water in the bottom of a **stove-top** pot and bring to a full boil with the peas in the basket above. Cover and set timer for 2-3 minutes. Or **microwave** on high for 3-4 minutes, then let stand.

   3 cups frozen baby peas

   Sometimes I sprinkle a little cheddar cheese on top and broil it for a few minutes. It makes the top crunchy and the kids really like it this way. We also like hot pepper flakes to spice it up.

   cheddar cheese, light, shredded (optional)

   hot pepper flakes (optional)

   <u>Serves 4-6</u>

DINNER IS READY IN 30 MINUTES

Equipment List:

Large stove-top pot w/lid
Large lasagna or cake pan
Stove-top pot w/steamer basket
Medium stove-top pot
Colander
Cheese grater
Can opener
Whisk or fork
Measuring cups and spoons
Aluminum foil

Per serving:

Calories	432
Fat	10.3 g
Protein	26.9 g
Carbohydrate	58.1 g
Fiber	4.3 g
Sodium	303 mg

U.S. Food Exchanges:		Cdn. Food Choices:	
2 1/2	Starch	3	Carb
2	Meat-lean	3 1/2	Meat/Alt
2	Vegetable	1	Other
1/2	Fat		
1/2	Milk-low fat		

20
to
prep

Savory Pot Roast with Harvest Veggies

Instructions:

...the night before...
Take out equipment.

1. Combine beef broth, asparagus soup, onion flakes, and spice together in your **slow cooker**. Stir.

   Place roast inside center pot of slow cooker and spoon sauce all over top of roast. Cover and leave in **fridge** overnight.

   ...in the morning...
   Return covered center pot to the outside of **slow cooker**. Set at **low heat**.
   It's meant to cook for about 8 hours.

   ...when you arrive home...
2. Rinse baby potatoes in a colander. Place potatoes and carrots together in a **stove-top** pot containing enough water to cover the vegetables.

   Bring to a full boil on high heat. Once boiling, **reduce heat** to a low boil. Set timer for 20 minutes or until veggies are tender.

3. Remove roast from **slow cooker**.

   Stir gravy mix with water in coffee mug. Blend into slow cooker juices using a fork or a whisk until it starts to thicken.
   If you like your gravy very thick...you will need to do this step in a stove-top pot at a higher heat.

Ingredients:

Take out ingredients.

1 can beef broth, reduced-sodium
(10 fl oz or 284 mL)
1 can cream of asparagus soup
(10 fl oz or 284 mL)
2 Tbsp onion flakes
1 Tbsp garlic & herb seasoning, salt-free

2-3 lbs or 900-1350 g sirloin
or round roast, boneless, trimmed
You can double the size of the roast, without increasing the other ingredients, to have leftovers or great lunch meat.

20 baby potatoes (or cut 4 large)
1 lb or 450 g washed baby carrots (or 4 large carrots peeled and cut into chunks)

3 Tbsp dry brown gravy mix combined with
3 Tbsp water *I like Bisto.*

This has got to be one of my all time favorite weeknight entertaining meals. Add a great salad and guests will moan and groan and think you've gone all out! My mouth is having a fit!!!!

Serves 4-6

DINNER IS READY IN 35 MINUTES

Equipment List:

...the night before...
Slow cooker
Can opener
Stirring spoon
Measuring spoons

...when you get home...
Large stove-top pot
Colander
Stirring spoon
Fork or whisk
Coffee mug
Measuring spoons

Per serving:

Calories	399
Fat	11.5 g
Protein	32.5 g
Carbohydrate	41.3 g
Fiber	5.1 g
Sodium	804 mg

U.S. Food Exchanges:		Cdn. Food Choices:	
2	Starch	2	Carb
4	Meat-lean	4 1/2	Meat/Alt
1 1/2	Vegetable	1/2	Other

15
to
prep

W
E
E
K

2

Thai Chicken Pizza with Veggie Toss

Instructions:

Don't change yet! Take out equipment.

1. Preheat **oven** to 350° F.

   Heat oil in a small nonstick **fry pan** or wok at med-high. Cut chicken into small bite size pieces and add to pan as you cut. Toss until chicken is no longer pink.
   Sprinkle with spice and set aside.

   Soften peanut butter, in a coffee mug, in the **microwave** for approx 15-25 seconds. Stir in soy sauce, water and cayenne. *Keep blending with a fork or a whisk until slightly runny.* You may have to add a tiny bit more water.

   Spread sauce over pizza crust.
   Top with sautéed chicken.
   Wash and finely chop green onion. Wash and slice mushrooms. Scatter both green onion and mushrooms over pizza base.
   Top with mozzarella cheese.

   Bake in **preheated oven**. Set timer for 5 min.

   ...meanwhile...
2. Rinse cold veggies in a colander. Place in serving bowl and drizzle with balsamic vinegar and olive oil.
   Toss veggies and set aside on table.

   ...when timer rings for pizza...
3. Change oven setting to **broil**. **Watch carefully**. When cheese begins to bubble, the pizza is ready.

   Rinse bean sprouts in a colander under cold water. Place onto a paper towel and pat dry. Remove pizza from the oven and sprinkle uncooked bean sprouts over top.

Ingredients:

Take out ingredients.

1 tsp canola or extra-virgin olive oil
1 chicken breast, boneless, skinless
 (1/3 lb or 150 g)
1/2 tsp hot chili flakes (optional)
1/2 tsp curry powder

3 Tbsp peanut butter, light
2 Tbsp soy sauce, reduced-sodium
1 Tbsp water
1/4 tsp cayenne (optional)

12" pizza crust (1/2 lb or 225 g)
 (pre-made from the bakery section)
3 green onions
6 mushrooms

1 cup mozzarella cheese, part-skim, shredded

1 lb or 450 g cut veggie mixture
 (e.g. carrots, cauliflower, broccoli, celery)
1 tsp balsamic vinegar
1 tsp olive oil, extra-virgin

1 cup bean sprouts
paper towel

If you like things spicy, like we do, sprinkle with hot chili flakes.

Serves 4

DINNER IS READY IN 25 MINUTES

Equipment List:

Small nonstick fry pan or wok
Colander
Salad bowl
2 cutting boards
Coffee mug
Cheese grater
Sharp meat knife
Sharp veggie knife
Large stirring spoon
Large serving spoon
Fork or whisk
Spatula
Measuring cups and spoons
Paper towel

Per serving:

Calories	400
Fat	14.2 g
Protein	27.0 g
Carbohydrate	44.5 g
Fiber	5.8 g
Sodium	886 mg

W
E
E
K

2

U.S. Food Exchanges:		Cdn. Food Choices:	
2 1/2	Starch	3	Carb
3	Meat-lean	4	Meat/Alt
1	Vegetable		
1	Fat		

About the Recipes

Blue

This is a great feel good meal! One of the family's favorites. It looks a little soupy when you're making it, and it's meant to stay that way when it's hot. Remember, it's served on rice, so you can pour this amazing sauce over a bed of rice. If you are vegetarian, replace the chicken with strips of firm tofu or soy based chicken flavored strips.

Yellow

This is the junk food dish of the week. I have to admit, I really feel like a kid again when we have this meal. When you mix a little fresh fruit in with the fruit cocktail, it gives a fresh fruit flavor with way less cutting and chopping. In the summer, I may use all fresh fruit with this. If I'm in a real rush, I may only use the fruit cocktail. Look at your timeline and adjust accordingly. Vegetarians can replace the beef with veggie grind and it works just fine.

Red

This is a fabulous goulash. You would never know by the flavor that it's the rushed version. By the way, did you know that peas have more iron than green beans, and more fiber? Cool huh! I personally look for the baby peas; I think they taste more like fresh. If you're a vegetarian, this meal is just perfect using veggie grind.

Yellow

When Ron and I were on tour for our book *Getting Ya Through the Summer*, we stopped at a little place in Nova Scotia, Canada, called Fisherman's Wharf. There was a little restaurant there which served up seafood chowder daily. Let me tell you, Ron and I moaned through the entire experience!! When we arrived back home, we tried chowder after chowder recipe. With much fixing and playing, we came up with what we think isn't exactly their chowder...but pretty darn close. This is loaded with veggies, so it's a great stand alone meal. Tip: if you ever want to freeze anything with a milk base, just remember all you have to do when you are reheating it is to add a little paste of cornstarch and milk, whisk it in and it brings it right back to life!

Green

This thigh dish has turned out to be one of my personal favorites. It's also fantastic served on rice.

Week 3

Blue: Layered Chicken with Rice and Broccoli

    Our family rating: 9
    Your family rating: _____

Yellow: Sloppy Beef on a Bun with Mixed Fruit

    Our family rating: 9
    Your family rating: _____

Red: Hurried Goulash
               with Egg Noodles and Peas

    Our family rating: 8.5
    Your family rating: _____

Yellow: Hearty Seafood Chowder with Salad

    Our family rating: 8.5
    Your family rating: _____

Green: Hot and Sour Chicken Thighs
               with Penne Pasta and Carrots

    Our family rating: 8.5
    Your family rating: _____

Layered Chicken with Rice and Broccoli

Instructions:

Don't change yet! Take out equipment.

1. Preheat **oven** to 350° F.
   Remove skin from roasted chicken. Peel cooked chicken off bones and cut into bite size pieces. Set aside.

   Mix soup, milk and spices together in a small bowl, in that order.
   Stir until smooth.

   Grate 2 cups cheddar cheese.

   Spray a large lasagna or cake pan with cooking spray. Layer 1/3 chicken, 1/3 sauce and 1/3 cheese. Do these layers two more times. Cover with aluminum foil and place in **preheated oven.** Set timer for 30 minutes.

2. Combine rice and water in a large microwave-safe pot with lid. **Microwave** at high 10 minutes, then medium 10 minutes.

   ...meanwhile...

3. Rinse broccoli in colander or steamer basket. Place a small amount of water in the bottom of a **stove-top** pot and bring to a full boil with the broccoli in the basket above. Cover and set timer for 3 minutes. ...or microwave at high for 3 minutes.
   Toss with butter if you must.

   Some of my family members like the layered chicken right on top of their rice and some like it on the side...either way, this is a great feel good meal.

Ingredients:

Take out ingredients.

1 pre-roasted chicken from the deli (2 lbs or 900 g)
(You end up with 1 lb or 450 g of meat.)

1 can cream of chicken soup, reduced-sodium (10 fl oz or 284 mL)
soup can filled with 1% milk
1/2 tsp fresh ground pepper
1 tsp garlic and herb seasoning, salt-free
1/2 tsp hot chili flakes (optional)
2 cups cheddar cheese, light shredded
Sometimes you can get cheese already grated for the same price.

cooking spray

aluminum foil

1 1/2 cups basmati or white rice
3 cups water

1 1/2 lbs or 675 g broccoli florets
water

butter (optional)

Serves 6-8

DINNER IS READY IN 45 MINUTES

Equipment List:

Large lasagna or cake pan
Large microwave-safe pot w/lid
Stove-top pot w/steamer basket
Salad spinner
Cutting board
Small mixing bowl
Can opener
Cheese grater
Sharp meat knife
Stirring spoons
Measuring cups and spoons
Aluminum foil

Per serving:

Calories	380
Fat	11.3 g
Protein	30.2 g
Carbohydrate	38.6 g
Fiber	1.0 g
Sodium	486 mg

U.S. Food Exchanges:		Cdn. Food Choices:	
2	Starch	2 1/2	Carb
4	Meat-lean	4	Meat/Alt
2	Vegetable		

20
to
prep

Sloppy Beef on a Bun with Mixed Fruit

Instructions:

Don't change yet! Take out equipment.

1. Preheat **oven** to 375° F.

2. Brown meat in a large nonstick **fry pan** at med-high until meat is no longer pink.
   Add onion flakes to pan.
   Add ketchup, prepared mustard, Worcestershire sauce and water to fully cooked meat.

   Stir, then **reduce heat** to a low simmer.

3. Slice buns and place them open side up on oven rack in **preheated oven**.
   Now, **turn oven off!**
   Crazy you say? No way, this is the most amazing way to warm buns in the oven.

   ...meanwhile...
4. Slice or cube your favorite seasonal fruit and mix together with fruit cocktail in a small bowl. *It looks great if you serve it in a short glass of some kind.*

   When you're ready to sit down and eat, spoon meat sauce onto warm bun.
   Top fruit cocktail with a spoonful of vanilla yogurt.

   Yuuuumy!!!!!

Ingredients:

Take out ingredients.

1 lb or 450 g ground beef, extra-lean

1 Tbsp onion flakes
1 cup ketchup
1 Tbsp prepared mustard
1 1/2 tsp Worcestershire sauce
1/2 cup water

4-6 hamburger buns, whole wheat
   Serve open faced or as a sloppy hamburger.

2 cups chopped seasonal fruit
   (e.g. oranges, grapes, cantaloupe)
1 can fruit salad, unsweetened (1 3/4 cups)

cheddar cheese, light, shredded (optional)

1/2 cup vanilla yogurt, low-fat
   (single serving size)

Serves 4-6

DINNER IS READY IN 25 MINUTES

Equipment List:

Large nonstick fry pan
Small bowl
Cutting board
Bread knife
Sharp veggie knife
Can opener
Stirring spoon
Serving spoon
Measuring cups and spoons

Per serving:

Calories	393
Fat	13.7 g
Protein	25.8 g
Carbohydrate	44.1 g
Fiber	4.2 g
Sodium	702 mg

U.S. Food Exchanges:		Cdn. Food Choices:	
2	Starch	2 1/2	Carb
3	Meat-lean	4	Meat/Alt
1	Fruit	1/2	Fat
1 1/2	Fat	1/2	Other

20 to prep

Hurried Goulash with Egg Noodles and Peas

Instructions:

Don't change yet! Take out equipment.

1. Fill a large **stove-top** pot with water and bring to a boil.

2. Heat oil in a large nonstick **fry pan** or wok at med-high. Cut beef into thin strips, against the grain, and add to pan as you cut. Toss occasionally.
   Cut onion into slivers. Add to pan as you cut. Add spices and toss.

   Wash and slice peppers into strips. Add to pan. Add garlic and olive oil.
   Toss until peppers look roasted.

   Add flour and stir. **Reduce heat** to med-low.

   Gradually stir in consommé and stewed tomatoes.

   Add chili flakes if you like it spicier.
   Mix together and heat through.

3. Place egg noodles in boiling water. Set timer according to package directions, approx 10 minutes.

4. Rinse peas in colander or steamer basket. Place a small amount of water in the bottom of a **stove-top** pot and bring to a full boil with the peas in the basket above. Cover and set timer for 2-3 minutes. Or **microwave** on high for 3-4 minutes, then let stand.

   ...when timer rings for noodles...
5. Rinse noodles in colander, return to pot and toss with a little olive oil if you wish.
   Serve meat sauce over egg noodles.

Ingredients:

Take out ingredients.

water

1 tsp olive oil, extra-virgin
1 1/2 lbs or 675 g lean sirloin
  (or flank steak)

1/2 red onion
2 Tbsp paprika (Hungarian is best)
1 tsp table blend seasoning, salt-free
1/4 tsp fresh ground pepper
1/2 red bell pepper
1/2 yellow bell pepper
1 or 2 tsp prepared garlic (from a jar)
  (or 1/2 tsp garlic powder)
1 tsp olive oil, extra-virgin
2 Tbsp flour

1 can beef consommé (10 fl oz or 284 mL)
1 can Italian stewed tomatoes
  (14 fl oz or 398 mL)
1 tsp hot chili flakes (optional)

3/4 lb or 340 g broad egg noodles
I like the "No Yolks" brand.
  (or use whole wheat noodles to increase your fiber intake)

3 cups frozen baby peas

olive oil (optional)

All ends well in the land of Goulash!

Serves 4-6

DINNER IS READY IN 30 MINUTES

Equipment List:

Large stove-top pot w/lid
Large nonstick fry-pan or wok
Stove-top pot w/steamer basket
Colander
2 cutting boards
Sharp meat knife
Sharp veggie knife
Large stirring spoon
Can opener
Serving spoon
Measuring cups and spoons

Per serving:

Calories	478
Fat	10.2 g
Protein	35.9 g
Carbohydrate	61.9g
Fiber	6.3 g
Sodium	595 mg

U.S. Food Exchanges:		Cdn. Food Choices:	
3	Starch	4	Carb
4	Meat-lean	5	Meat/Alt
2	Vegetable		

15 to prep

W
E
E
K

3

Hearty Seafood Chowder with Salad

Instructions:

Don't change yet! Take out equipment.

1. Melt butter with oil at med-low in a large **stove-top** pot.
    Wash and dice the following, adding to pot as you cut: potatoes, carrots, onion and celery.

    Add spices and garlic.

    Sprinkle with flour and stir until well coated.

    Gradually add chicken broth, stirring constantly as you add. **Bring to a boil then reduce to a low boil at medium heat.**
    Set timer for 12 minutes. (or until you are almost able to slice through a carrot or potato).

    … meanwhile…
2. Break lettuce directly into salad spinner and spin dry. Slice any leftover veggies or peppers you have on hand.
    Serve with your favorite salad dressing.

    ...when timer rings...
3. Add scallops and crab into pot and when broth returns to a low boil set timer for 3 minutes.

    ...when timer rings again...
4. Add milk (potatoes should be tender) and heat through.

Ingredients:

Take out ingredients.

2 Tbsp butter
2 Tbsp olive oil, extra-virgin
4 large potatoes
3 carrots
1 onion
4 celery ribs
1/4 tsp pepper
1 tsp Mrs. Dash Original Seasoning
2 tsp prepared garlic (from a jar)
1/2 cup flour

8 cups chicken broth, reduced-sodium

1 head green leaf lettuce
1 cup leftover veggies (tomatoes, peppers)

5 Tbsp salad dressing, light

1/2 lb or 225 g frozen or fresh scallops
1 can of crab or lobster meat, drained (6 oz or 170 g)

1 1/2 cups 1% milk

multigrain bread (optional)

Serves 6-8

DINNER IS READY IN 30 MINUTES

Equipment List:

Large stove-top pot
2 cutting boards
Salad spinner
Salad tongs
Can opener
Soup ladle
Large stirring spoon
Sharp veggie knife
Measuring cups and spoons

Per serving:

Calories	294
Fat	8.9 g
Protein	17.1 g
Carbohydrate	37.4 g
Fiber	4.9 g
Sodium	815 mg

U.S. Food Exchanges:		Cdn. Food Choices:	
1	Starch	2	Carb
2	Meat-lean	2 1/2	Meat/Alt
2	Vegetable	1/2	Fat
1/2	Fat		
1/2	Milk-low fat		

20 to prep

W
E
E
K

3

Hot & Sour Chicken Thighs with Penne Pasta and Carrots

Instructions:

Don't change yet! Take out equipment.

1. Preheat **oven** to 350º F.
   Unravel thighs to flatten and scrunch together in a large lasagna or cake pan.

   Mix together Catalina dressing, cranberry sauce, onion flakes, pepper and spice in a bowl. Pour sauce evenly over chicken.

   Bake in **preheated oven**.
   Set timer for 40 minutes.

2. Rinse carrots in colander under cold water. Place in a microwave-safe pot or casserole dish with lid. Cover and **microwave** at high for 5 minutes, then let stand.

3. Fill a large **stove-top** pot with water. Let stand.

   ...when timer rings for chicken...
   Turn off heat and leave it in the oven.
   Bring water for pasta to a boil.
   Add pasta to boiling water.
   Set timer according to package directions, approx 11 minutes. Stir occasionally.

   ...when timer rings for pasta...
   Drain and rinse pasta in a colander under hot water. Return pasta to pot, **no heat**, and toss with a little olive oil and spice if you wish.

4. **Microwave** carrots at high for 2 additional minutes.

   Diiiiinner is ready!!!

Ingredients:

Take out ingredients.

chicken thighs, boneless, skinless (1 3/4 lbs or 800 g)

1 cup Catalina salad dressing, low-fat
3/4 cup whole cranberry sauce
If you have extra, freeze the rest in a freezer bag for the next time.
2 Tbsp onion flakes
1/4 tsp fresh ground pepper
1 1/2 tsp table blend seasoning, salt-free

1 lb or 450 g frozen baby carrots

3/4 lb or 340 g penne pasta, whole wheat

olive oil, extra-virgin (optional)
basil leaves (optional)

<u>Serves 4-6</u>

DINNER IS READY IN 60 MINUTES

Equipment List:

Large stove-top pot
Large lasagna or cake pan
Microwave-safe pot w/lid
Colander
Mixing bowl
Can opener
Stirring spoon
Measuring cups and spoons

Per serving:

Calories	482
Fat	7.5 g
Protein	35.5 g
Carbohydrate	71.9 g
Fiber	7.7 g
Sodium	608 mg

20 to prep

U.S. Food Exchanges:		Cdn. Food Choices:	
2 1/2	Starch	3 1/2	Carb
4	Meat-lean	5	Meat/Alt
1	Vegetable	1	Other
1	Other Carb		

About the Recipes

Yellow

This is definitely my favorite chicken stew. This meal-in-one still can please those picky eaters because the chunks are big and easy to pick out. If you are vegetarian, you can either make this a total veggie stew and have some type of protein on the side or you can throw in chunks of firm tofu or canned mixed beans or lentils then let it simmer in the sauce for a bit.

Blue

This is an amazing roast with a really interesting flavor. I like to add a little zip in the form of hot sauce or chili flakes to give even more of a kick. If you serve this very easy roast to guests, you'll get lots of compliments.

Red

A ten from my family! I have teens who will decide to stay home for dinner on the weekend (and invite a few friends over) for this meal. Here's a tip: if I'm really pressed for time, I don't bother skewering the chicken. I do everything else the same and just broil the chicken on a sprayed broiler pan. If you are using a BBQ, you can now get aluminum foil trays with holes; it works great for these. I do give a shot of cooking spray first. If you are a devout vegetarian you can use fried tofu cubes. Not my favorite, but tofu lovers will enjoy it.

Yellow

This is the junk food meal of the week. Kids go nuts over this. It really has a delicious flavor. If you are vegetarian, veggie grind works great!

Green

Okay, reeeeeeeeeeeeally good! I just love this meal! I'm often asked if a person can just go ahead and replace chicken thighs with chicken breast. I choose thighs for certain meals because I love how moist they are with the sauce. The nutritional data is still excellent. Many people prefer to use breast. Go right ahead. Same great flavor, the meat's just not as moist!

Week 4

Yellow:

Amazing Chicken Stew on Rice

Our family rating: 10
Your family rating: _____

Blue:

Tangy Slow Cooker Roast
with Potatoes and Peas

Our family rating: 8.5
Your family rating: _____

Red:

Peanut Satay Chicken Kabobs
with Spinach Salad

Our family rating: 10
Your family rating: _____

Yellow:

Macaroni Lasagna with Veggies and Dip

Our family rating: 9
Your family rating: _____

Green:

Dijon Baked Chicken with Rice and Broccoli

Our family rating: 9.5
Your family rating: _____

Amazing Chicken Stew on Rice

Instructions:

Don't change yet! Take out equipment.

1. Combine rice and water in a large microwave-safe pot with lid. **Microwave** at high 10 minutes, then medium 10 minutes.

2. Spray a large heavy **stove-top** pot with cooking spray.
Cut chicken into bite size pieces and add to pan as you cut. Cook at med-high.
Toss until meat is no longer pink.

Add spices and Worcestershire sauce. Stir.

Chop onion, slice celery and mushrooms. Add to pan as you cut.

Rinse broccoli and carrots in a colander and add to pan.

Add soup and gradually stir in water.

Simmer until hot and flavors have combined, approx 15 minutes.
Check to make sure you can poke through a carrot with a fork.

Serve stew over rice.

Ingredients:

Take out ingredients.

1 1/2 cups basmati or white rice
3 cups water

cooking spray

3 chicken breasts, boneless, skinless
 (1 lb or 450 g)

1 tsp lemon pepper
1/4 tsp fresh pepper
1/4 tsp garlic and herb seasoning, salt-free
2 tsp Worcestershire Sauce

1 onion
3 celery ribs
12 mushrooms
3 cups frozen broccoli florets
 (3/4 lb or 340 g)
2 cups frozen baby carrots (1/2 lb or 225 g)
1 can cream of chicken soup, reduced-sodium (10 fl oz or 284 mL)
1 cup water

Serves 6

DINNER IS READY IN 30 MINUTES

Equipment List:

Large microwave-safe pot w/lid
Large stove-top pot
Colander
2 cutting boards
Sharp meat knife
Sharp veggie knife
Can opener
Fork
Measuring cups and spoons

Per serving:

Calories	351
Fat	3.4 g
Protein	26.0 g
Carbohydrate	54.4 g
Fiber	6.2 g
Sodium	431 mg

U.S. Food Exchanges:		Cdn. Food Choices:	
2 1/2	Starch	3	Carb
3	Meat-lean	4	Meat/Alt
2	Vegetable		

20 to prep

Tangy Slow Cooker Roast with Potatoes and Peas

Instructions:

...the night before...
Take out equipment.

1. Place frozen roast inside center pot of **slow-cooker**. Sprinkle the spice and onion flakes over top.

   Spoon cranberry sauce over top of roast. Cover and leave in **fridge** overnight.

   ...in the morning...
   Return centre pot, with cover, to outer liner of slow-cooker. Set on **low heat**.

   ...when you arrive home...
2. Wash potatoes and place in a large **stove-top** pot with cold water. Bring to a full boil on high heat. Once boiling, **reduce heat** to a low boil. Set timer for 15 minutes or until you can slide a knife into the potato easily.

3. Rinse peas in colander or steamer basket. Place a small amount of water in the bottom of a **stove-top** pot and bring to a full boil with the peas in the basket above. Cover and set timer for 2-3 minutes. Or **microwave** on high for 3-4 minutes, then let stand.

4. Remove roast from slow-cooker.

   Stir gravy mix with water in coffee mug. Blend into slow-cooker juices using a fork or a whisk until it starts to thicken.
   Slice roast and cover with foil to keep warm.

Ingredients:

Take out ingredients.

2-3 lbs rump roast (fat trimmed)
2 tsp table blend seasoning, salt-free
2 Tbsp onion flakes

3/4 cup whole berry cranberry sauce
If you have some left over, you can toss it in a freezer bag and freeze it for the next time.

20 baby potatoes (or cut 4 large)
water

3 cups frozen baby peas
water

3 Tbsp dry brown gravy mix combined with
3 Tbsp water *I like Bisto.*

aluminum foil

<u>**Serves 4-6**</u>

DINNER IS READY IN 35 MINUTES

Equipment List:

...the night before...
Slow cooker
Can opener
Spoon
Measuring cups and spoons
...when you get home...
Large stove-top pot
Stove-top pot w/steamer basket
Colander
Coffee mug
Fork or whisk
Knife
Spoon
Measuring cups and spoons
Aluminum foil

Per serving:

Calories	476
Fat	11.9 g
Protein	38.8 g
Carbohydrate	53.6 g
Fiber	6.9 g
Sodium	330 mg

U.S. Food Exchanges:	Cdn. Food Choices:
2 1/2 Starch	2 1/2 Carb
4 1/2 Meat-lean	4 1/2 Meat/Alt
1 Vegetable	1 Other
1 Other Carb	

20 to prep

Peanut Satay Chicken Kabobs with Multigrain Buns and Spinach Salad

Instructions:

Don't change yet! Take out equipment.

1. Soak your skewers in warm water while you're preparing the meal. It makes it a lot easier to skewer the meat.

   Cut chicken into cubes (approx 1 1/2" x 1 1/2"). Toss into a resealable plastic bag. Pour peanut satay sauce all over. Close bag and smoosh together. Let stand in **fridge**.

2. Rinse spinach under cold water in a salad spinner. Spin dry. Arrange on plates. Wash and slice strawberries. Arrange on top of spinach. *Add croutons if you like.*

3. Set oven to **broil**.
   Spray a broiler pan with cooking spray. Skewer chicken onto skewers leaving a small space between each piece of chicken. *Simply place the cubes onto the broiler pan if you don't have time to skewer them.*

   Turn chicken cubes as they brown. Watch them carefully. Chicken is ready when the inside of the largest piece is white (160° F).

   Arrange skewers of chicken beside salad.

4. Drizzle dressing on salad.

5. Serve with multigrain buns.

   I also like to have a little bowl of sesame seeds on the table. Ron and I like to drizzle a little satay sauce on the meat and then sprinkle a few sesame seeds on top. Nuuuummmmy!!!

Ingredients:

Take out ingredients.

4-6 bamboo skewers (can be found in gadget section of grocery store)

4 chicken breasts, boneless, skinless (1 1/2 lbs or 675 g)
1 large plastic resealable bag
1/2 cup bottled peanut satay sauce (or Szechwan sauce)

12 oz or 340 g pre-washed baby spinach

6 strawberries
1/2 cup croutons (optional)
If you have the time make the candied nuts on the back flap.

cooking spray

Have the peanut satay sauce on the table for extra dipping if you like. Use a low-fat variety to reduce your fat intake.

1/4 cup raspberry vinaigrette, low-fat

6-8 multigrain buns
butter (optional)

sesame seeds (optional)

<u>**Serves 4-6**</u>

DINNER IS READY IN 30 MINUTES

Equipment List:

Broiler pan or BBQ grill
Bamboo skewers
Cutting board
Salad spinner
Salad tongs
Serving plates
Sharp meat knife
Resealable plastic bag
Measuring cups and spoons

Per serving:

Calories	351
Fat	11.6 g
Protein	35.2 g
Carbohydrate	27.4 g
Fiber	3.9 g
Sodium	407 mg

U.S. Food Exchanges:		Cdn. Food Choices:	
1 1/2	Starch	2	Carb
4	Meat-lean	4	Meat/Alt
1	Vegetable		

Macaroni Lasagna with Veggies and Dip

Instructions:

Don't change yet! Take out equipment.

1. Preheat **oven** to 375° F.

2. Fill a large **stove-top** pot with water and bring to boil.

3. Brown meat in a large nonstick **fry pan** at med-high until meat is no longer pink. Add onion flakes and spices while meat is browning.

4. Place macaroni in boiling water. Cook for 5 minutes. You want the pasta very firm.

    …meanwhile…

5. Mix together mayonnaise, sour cream and spice in a small mixing bowl to make veggie dip. Let stand in **fridge**.

    Rinse veggies and arrange on a serving plate.

    …when timer rings for pasta...

6. Rinse pasta in colander and let drain.

7. Layer the following ingredients into a large lasagna or cake pan in this order: 1/2 of the fully cooked beef, 1/2 of the cooked macaroni, 1/2 pasta sauce and 1/2 cheese. Repeat.

    Bake uncovered in **preheated oven**.
    Set timer for 20 minutes or until top layer of cheese is bubbly.

    Set the table…and dinner is served!

Ingredients:

Take out ingredients.

water

1 lb or 450 g ground beef, extra-lean
1 Tbsp onion flakes
1 tsp Italian seasoning
1 tsp hot chili flakes (optional)

2 1/2 cups macaroni, whole wheat

1/2 cup mayonnaise, light
1/2 cup sour cream, no-fat
1/2 tsp garlic and herb seasoning, salt-free

1 1/2 lbs or 675 g precut veggies
(approx 6 cups celery, cauliflower, broccoli and carrots)

prepared cooked beef
prepared cooked macaroni
1 can of your favorite pasta sauce
(24 fl oz or 680 mL)
I use spicy tomato blend.
2 cups cheddar cheese, light, shredded

<u>**Serves 6-8**</u>

DINNER IS READY IN 25 MINUTES

Equipment List:

Large nonstick fry pan
Large stove-top pot
Large lasagna or cake pan
Colander
Small mixing bowl
Serving plate
Small stirring spoon
2 large stirring spoons
Measuring cups and spoons

Per serving:

Calories	426
Fat	17.4 g
Protein	25.5 g
Carbohydrate	42.4 g
Fiber	6.4 g
Sodium	617 mg

U.S. Food Exchanges:		Cdn. Food Choices:	
2	Starch	2 1/2	Carb
3	Meat-lean	3	Meat/Alt
2	Vegetable	1 1/2	Fat
2	Fat		

20 to prep

Dijon Baked Chicken with Rice and Broccoli

Instructions:

...the night before...
Take out equipment.

1. Unravel thighs to flatten and scrunch together in a large lasagna or cake pan.

   Combine the following in a small mixing bowl in this order: spices, honey, Dijon mustard, soy sauce and chili paste. Stir.

   Pour evenly over chicken. Flip the chicken around with a fork until each piece is well coated. End by making sure the rough side of the thigh is down.
   Cover with plastic wrap and **refrigerate** overnight.

   ...when you arrive home...
2. Preheat **oven** to 350° F.

3. Combine rice and water in a large oven-safe pot. Stir. Cover and place in **preheated oven**.

4. Turn chicken over with a fork. Place in **preheated oven**, beside rice.
   Set timer for 50 minutes.
   About half way through the cooking time for chicken, I like to flip the chicken over again.

   ...when timer rings for chicken...
   Turn off heat but leave it in the oven.

5. Rinse broccoli in colander or steamer basket. Place a small amount of water in the bottom of a **stove-top** pot and bring to a full boil with the broccoli in the basket above. Cover and set timer for 3 minutes. ...or microwave at high for 3 minutes.
   When timer rings toss with butter and spice.

Ingredients:

Take out ingredients.

chicken thighs, boneless, skinless
  (1 3/4 lbs or 800 g)

1 Tbsp curry powder
1 Tbsp onion flakes
1/2 tsp hot chili flakes (optional)
1/2 cup liquid honey
1/2 cup Dijon mustard
2 Tbsp soy sauce, reduced-sodium
1 tsp Sambal Oelek (crushed chili paste)

plastic wrap

1 1/2 cups basmati or white rice
3 cups water

If you forget to marinate this overnight, don't worry; it's still great if you cook the chicken in the sauce as soon as you make it. It's just better when it marinates!

1 lb or 450 g broccoli florets
water

butter (optional)
1/4 tsp table blend seasoning, salt-free

Serves 4-6

DINNER IS READY IN 60 MINUTES

Equipment List:

...the night before...

Large lasagna or cake pan
Small mixing bowl
Stirring spoon
Fork
Measuring cups and spoons
Plastic wrap

...when you get home...

Large oven-safe pot w/lid
Stove-top pot w/steamer basket
Colander
Fork
Stirring spoon
Measuring cups and spoons

Per serving:

Calories	448
Fat	7.0 g
Protein	32.7 g
Carbohydrate	65.2 g
Fiber	2.1 g
Sodium	585 mg

U.S. Food Exchanges:		Cdn. Food Choices:	
3	Starch	4	Carb
3	Meat-very lean	3 1/2	Meat/Alt
2	Vegetable	1/2	Other
1	Fat		
1/2	Other Carb		

About the Recipes

Red

My kids consider this to be the junk food meal of the week. I was never a big fan of cheese tortellini, but my family loves it. It was literally a mission of mine to find ways to make tortellini dishes that I would actually like. Now, it's one of my favorites. I like things a little spicier, so I always add chili flakes to mine. Vegetarians: Take out the chicken step and it's just as good without.

Yellow

These meatballs have such a lovely flavor. I'm always asked by people what to do when an Asian or Polynesian dish includes pineapple, but there aren't pineapple fans in the family. Just purchase the large slices, because the juice is usually really important for the flavor. It's often the texture of pineapple in a dish that people don't like. I have to say, I'm a little like that myself. Make up the recipe and then just serve the slices on the side. You'll be amazed how many more people like cold pineapple slices, as opposed to cut up cooked pineapple.

Blue

The flavor of this thigh dish is quite unusual. The cider vinegar and Dijon really give it a nice punch! I also love to serve this meal on rice...in fact, it's a toss up which I like more.

Green

Oh yeah! Ok! I could eat this once a week. Don't be shy to try this with rice as well. It's amazing. Now, the trick to this is not discarding the juices that collect from the salmon. You can really cut down on the amount of dressing you use when you pour those drippings from the foil into a gravy bowl. We're learning how amazing salmon is for our bodies. Believe me, the flavor of this is also goooood for your soul!!! Great for entertaining? Oh, yes!!!

Yellow

This is a fabulous slow cooker soup. I don't fret if I don't have the canned milk; I use regular and it's just fine. I do caution you not to put the rice in ahead of time or it gets really mushy. If you put it in 20 minutes before you're about to eat, it's perfect. If you're vegetarian, you can make this meatless. Use vegetable broth instead of chicken broth. Don't forget to have a side of protein!

Week 5

Red: Chicken and Mushroom Tortellini
with Veggies and Dip

Our family rating: 9.5
Your family rating: _____

Yellow: Chinese Meatballs on Rice
with Peas and Pea Pods

Our family rating: 8
Your family rating: _____

Blue: Oven BBQ Chicken
with Roast Potatoes and Broccoli

Our family rating: 9.5
Your family rating: _____

Green: Asian Salmon with Bird's Nest Pasta
and Asparagus

Our family rating: 10
Your family rating: _____

Yellow: Creamy Chicken and Rice Soup
with Multigrain Buns

Our family rating: 9.5
Your family rating: _____

5

Chicken and Mushroom Tortellini with Veggies and Dip

Instructions:

Don't change yet! Take out equipment.

1. Heat oil in a large **stove-top** pot at medium. Cut chicken into bite size pieces and add to pot as you cut. Season with spice and stir until meat is no longer pink.

   Dice onion and slice celery adding to pot as you cut.
   Rinse and slice mushrooms. Add to pot.

   Add mushroom soup and stir.
   Gradually add chicken broth and stir.
   Add milk to pot and stir.

   Add tortellini to pot. **Reduce heat** to simmer. Set timer for 15 minutes or until tortellini is soft. **Stir often.**

2. Rinse veggies and arrange on a plate.

   Combine mayonnaise, sour cream and spice in a small mixing bowl. Stir and set aside.

   This may look a little watered down while you're making it…but the tortellini ends up puffing up and the sauce ends up being just perfect. A little Parmesan on this is delicious!

Ingredients:

Take out ingredients.

1 tsp canola oil
3 chicken breasts, boneless, skinless
 (1 lb or 450 g)
1 tsp garlic powder
1/2 tsp hot chili flakes (optional)

1/2 onion
1 celery rib
5 mushrooms

1 can mushroom soup, reduced-sodium
 (10 fl oz or 284 mL)
1 can chicken broth, reduced-sodium
 (10 fl oz or 284 mL)
2 cups 1% milk

4 1/2 cups cheese tortellini
 (from the deli or dairy dept)

1 lb or 450 g precut veggies
 (4 cups celery, cauliflower, carrots, broccoli)

Veggie Dip
1/2 cup mayonnaise, light
1/2 cup sour cream, no-fat
1 tsp garlic & herb seasoning, salt-free

Parmesan cheese, light, grated (optional)

Serves 4-6

DINNER IS READY IN 30 MINUTES

Equipment List:

Large stove-top pot
2 cutting boards
Colander
Small mixing bowl
Serving plate
Sharp meat knife
Sharp veggie knife
Large stirring spoon
Small stirring spoon
Cheese grater
Can opener
Measuring cups and spoons

Per serving:

Calories	493
Fat	15.7 g
Protein	34.3 g
Carbohydrate	53.9 g
Fiber	3.5 g
Sodium	869 mg

U.S. Food Exchanges:		Cdn. Food Choices:	
2 1/2	Starch	3	Carb
3	Meat-lean	3 1/2	Meat/Alt
2	Vegetable	1	Fat
1	Fat	1/2	Other
1/2	Milk-low fat		

15 to prep

WEEK 5

Chinese Meatballs on Rice
with Peas and Pea Pods

Instructions:	Ingredients:
Don't change yet! Take out equipment.	Take out ingredients.

1. Form 1" meatballs and add to a large **fry pan** at med heat, as you form.

    1 1/2 lbs or 675 g ground beef, extra-lean

    Flip meatballs over to brown other side.
    Add garlic and spices to pan.

    2 tsp prepared garlic (from a jar)
    1/2 tsp table blend seasoning, salt-free
    1/4 tsp fresh ground pepper
    1 green bell pepper
      (or use 1/2 red and 1/2 green)

    Wash and chop pepper into small chunks, adding to pan as you cut.

    Measure cornstarch into a 2 cup measuring cup or bowl. Add 1 cup of juice from the can of pineapple into the cornstarch, stirring as you add. Set aside pineapple chunks.
    Add vinegar, then pour this liquid over fully cooked meatballs.

    2 Tbsp cornstarch
    1 cup pineapple juice
      (juice from a can of unsweetened pineapple
      chunks, 20 fl oz or 540 mL can size)
    2 Tbsp vinegar

    In the uncleaned measuring cup combine sugar, beef broth and soy sauce.
    Pour mixture into pan.

    1/2 cup brown sugar
    1 cup beef broth, reduced-sodium
      (or use chicken broth)
    1 Tbsp soy sauce, reduced-sodium
    1 1/4 cups of reserved pineapple chunks
      (set remainder of pineapple aside)

    Add pineapple chunks to pan.
    Reduce heat to a high simmer.

2. Combine rice and water in a large microwave-safe pot with lid. **Microwave** at high 10 minutes.

    1 1/2 cups basmati or white rice
    3 cups water

    ...when timer rings for rice...
    Add peas and pea pods to rice. Stir and return rice to microwave for 10 minutes on medium heat.

    10 oz or 300 g frozen pea pods
    1 cup frozen baby peas

    Serve the meatballs with the rice and use the remaining pineapple as a garnish.

    remaining pineapple chunks (optional)

    Serves 4-6

DINNER IS READY IN 25 MINUTES

Equipment List:

Large nontick fry pan
Large microwave-safe pot w/lid
Cutting board
2 cup measuring cup or bowl
Can opener
Sharp veggie knife
2 large stirring spoons
Measuring cups and spoons

Per serving:

Calories	499
Fat	12.6 g
Protein	27.0 g
Carbohydrate	68.8 g
Fiber	4.3 g
Sodium	291 mg

U.S. Food Exchanges:		Cdn. Food Choices:	
2 1/2	Starch	3 1/2	Carb
3	Meat-lean	3	Meat/Alt
2	Vegetable	1	Fat
1	Fruit	1	Other
1	Fat		

Oven BBQ Chicken
with Roast Potatoes and Broccoli

Instructions:

Don't change yet! Take out equipment.

1. Preheat **oven** to 350° F.
    Unravel thighs and lay flat in a large lasagna
    or cake pan.

    Finely chop onion.
    Combine the following in a small bowl in this
    order: onion, brown sugar, vinegar, tomato
    sauce, garlic, mustard and spices.
    Stir, then pour evenly over chicken.

    Place in **preheated oven**.
    Set timer for 50 minutes.

2. Wash potatoes and place in a different large
    lasagna or cake pan.
    Toss with olive oil and spice until potatoes are
    coated.
    Place in **preheated oven** beside chicken.

    ...when timer rings for chicken...

3. Rinse broccoli in colander or steamer basket.
    Place a small amount of water in the bottom
    of a **stove-top** pot and bring to a full boil with
    the broccoli in the basket above. Cover and set
    timer for 3 minutes. ...or microwave at high
    for 3 minutes.
    Toss with butter if you must.

Ingredients:

Take out ingredients.

**chicken thighs, boneless, skinless
 (1 3/4 lbs or 800 g)**

1 onion

1/2 cup brown sugar
1/2 cup cider vinegar
**1 can tomato sauce, no salt added
 (14 fl oz or 398 mL)**
2 tsp prepared garlic (in a jar)
1/3 cup Dijon mustard
1 Tbsp Italian seasoning
1/4-1/2 tsp cayenne pepper

20 baby potatoes
 (or cut 4 large potatoes)
2 tsp olive oil, extra-virgin
1 tsp Mrs. Dash Original Seasoning

**1 lb or 450 g broccoli florets
water**

butter (optional)

Serves 4-6

DINNER IS READY IN 60 MINUTES

Equipment List:

2 large lasagna or cake pans
Stove top pot w/steamer basket
Colander
Small mixing bowl
Cutting board
Sharp veggie knife
2 stirring spoons
Can opener
Measuring cups and spoons

Per serving:

Calories	428
Fat	7.9 g
Protein	33.1 g
Carbohydrate	58.4 g
Fiber	5.2 g
Sodium	326 mg

U.S. Food Exchanges:

2 1/2	Starch
3	Meat-lean
2	Vegetable
1/2	Other Carb

Cdn. Food Choices:

3	Carb
3 1/2	Meat/Alt
1/2	Other

20 to prep

WEEK 5

Asian Salmon with Bird's Nest Pasta and Asparagus

Instructions:

Don't change yet! Take out equipment.

1. Preheat **oven** to 350° F.
    Spray a nonstick **fry pan** with cooking spray. Wash salmon under cold water, pat dry with paper towel and season one side. Sauté, spice side down, over med-heat approx 1 minute. Season, turn and sauté other side.

    …while salmon is searing…
    Wet the outside of a paper bag thoroughly under cold water. Spray a large piece of aluminum foil, shiny side up, with cooking spray.

    Arrange the seared filets on the foil. Drizzle sauce onto each piece. Turn the edges of foil up to prevent leaking. Pull the foil into the inside of the wet bag. Curl the end of the bag tightly and place in **preheated oven** on center rack. Set timer for 25 minutes.

2. Fill a large **stove-top** pot with water and bring to a boil.
    …meanwhile…

3. Snap off bottom nodes of asparagus and discard. Rinse in colander or steamer basket. Place a small amount of water in the bottom of a **stove-top** pot and bring to a full boil with the asparagus in the basket above. Cover and set timer for 4 minutes…or microwave for the same amount of time.
    ...when timer rings for asparagus...
    Drain water. Toss in pot with butter and salt.

4. Cook pasta for recommended time, approx 4 minutes. Gently drain in colander.
    I like to drizzle sesame oil in the empty cooking pot and place the bird's nests back in the pot. I swirl them gently in the oil then cover to keep them warm.

5. Place hot salmon on noodles directly on serving plate. Combine salmon drippings from foil with additional sauce. Stir and drizzle over salmon and noodles.

Ingredients:

Take out ingredients.

cooking spray
4 salmon filets, boneless, skinless (pink)
  (6 oz or 170 g each)
paper towel
1/4 tsp Mrs. Dash Original Seasoning
  per fillet

medium size paper bag (grocery type)
heavy aluminum foil
cooking spray

1/4 cup Thai peanut sauce
  (can be Szechuan or peanut satay)

water

20 asparagus spears (1 lb or 450 g)

water

1 tsp butter (optional)
pinch of salt (optional)

8 bird's nest pasta bundles **(3/4 lb or 340 g)**
  (often found in your grocer's specialty food department)
1 tsp sesame oil (optional)

2 Tbsp Thai peanut sauce
  (can be Szechuan or peanut satay)

Serves 4-6

DINNER IS READY IN 40 MINUTES

Equipment List:

Large nonstick fry pan
Large stove-top pot
Stove top pot w/steamer basket
Colander
Flipper
Measuring cups and spoons
Paper towel
Medium weight paper bag
Aluminum foil

Per serving:

Calories	422
Fat	10.3 g
Protein	34.0 g
Carbohydrate	48.4 g
Fiber	3.5 g
Sodium	129 mg

U.S. Food Exchanges:		Cdn. Food Choices:	
3	Starch	3	Carb
3 1/2	Meat-lean	3 1/2	Meat/Alt
1	Vegetable		

15 to prep

Creamy Chicken and Rice Soup with Multigrain Buns

Instructions:

...the night before...
Take out equipment.

1. Dice onion, cut carrots and slice celery. Place in the inside pot of **slow cooker**.
   If you have an onion hater in your house, saute until caramelized before adding to pot.
   Microwave butter in a small cup for 5 seconds. Pour butter over veggies and stir to coat.
   Stir in spices and flour.

   Gradually add chicken broth stirring constantly to avoid lumping.
   Add evaporated milk.

   Remove meat from 1/2 a roasted chicken. Cut into bite size chunks and add to slow cooker. Stir, cover and store in **fridge** overnight.

   ...in the morning...
   Return center pot with cover to the outer liner of slow cooker and set on **low heat**.

   ...when you arrive home...
   Toss in rice and stir well.
   Set timer for 20 minutes.
   If the sauce needs a little thickening, combine a small amount of dry gravy mix blended with water and stir in.

2. Serve with buns.

Ingredients:

Take out ingredients.

1/2 cup chopped onion (fresh or frozen)
3 carrots
2 celery ribs

1 Tbsp butter

1 Tbsp dried chives
1/4 tsp fresh ground pepper
1/2 tsp poultry seasoning
1 tsp Italian seasoning
1/4 cup flour

6 cups chicken broth, reduced-sodium

1 1/2 cups evaporated milk, low-fat

1/2 pre-roasted chicken from the deli
   (assumes 1 whole chicken = 2 lbs or 900 g and meat from 1/2 chicken = 1/2 lb or 225 g)
   Use the other half for lunch meat
   ...or throw in the freezer for future meals
   ...or buy deli cooked chicken breast.

3/4 cup basmati or white rice

2 Tbsp dry gravy mix combined with
2 Tbsp water (optional)
   I like Bisto.

6 multigrain buns

<u>Serves 6</u>

DINNER IS READY IN 30 MINUTES

Equipment List:

...the night before...

Slow cooker
Coffee mug
2 cutting boards
Sharp veggie knife
Sharp meat knife
Large stirring spoon
Can opener
Measuring cups and spoons

...when you get home...

Soup ladle
Measuring cups and spoons

Per serving:

Calories	398
Fat	8.9 g
Protein	24.9 g
Carbohydrate	54.5 g
Fiber	3.7 g
Sodium	890 mg

U.S. Food Exchanges:		Cdn. Food Choices:	
2 1/2	Starch	3 1/2	Carb
2	Meat-lean	2	Meat/Alt
1	Vegetable	1	Fat
1/2	Fat		
1/2	Milk-low fat		

20 to prep

About the Recipes

Yellow

Yup…this is one of my favorite recipes in the book. Ron and I really want to encourage people to do a few things to make a very simple meal a little gourmet. This meal is on the table, start to finish, in a little over 20 minutes--but I would entertain with it in a second. Why wait for company? Do neat stuff with your pasta dishes--serve them in bowls, stand up the asparagus, it doesn't take any longer, but it just looks neat. Have fun!!! If you're a vegetarian, this is great with firm tofu or as a stand alone sauce. Sprinkle some candied pecans or almonds on top for the added protein. (See back flap for recipe.)

Green

This is just a very plain fish and chip recipe. It also has about 1/2 of the fat you would normally have with deep fried fish. By the way, you can use an egg white and milk wash as well if you don't have buttermilk. Adults in our house love this with the spicy tartar sauce on the back flap; our kids plaster on the ketchup, oh well, they're eating fish!

Red

Really, really, really nice flavor. This started out with some ideas I got from a chef I worked with a few years back. The flavor is really amazing. Just a note: some people get turned off stroganoff because they hate blending sour cream in. Soooo…don't! This recipe is still amazing, sour cream or not. Vegetarians: Use veggie grind and it's just lovely!

Blue

This thigh dish is not too spicy, maybe with a little bit of an Asian flavor. Very tender, very amazing, and yes, go ahead and make it with chicken breast if you wish. It's just great. It's actually lovely with pork chops as well. You can also make this on the spot; it just has a more intense flavor when you make it the night before. So don't panic if you forgot to prepare ahead, you'll still be pleased with the results.

Yellow

This is the junk food meal of the week. My kids love to throw a whole variety of things on these. Salsa, cheese, tomatoes, peppers, onions, you name it. I have plenty of veggies cut up and ready to stuff. That way, the kids are happy and we're all getting our veggies. Vegetarians: Try making this with store bought falafels. Make sure you add the cheese for protein.

Week 6

Yellow:

Chicken in a Mango Cream Sauce on Pasta with Asparagus

Our family rating: 10
Your family rating: _____

Green:

Fish and Chips with Salad

Our family rating: 8
Your family rating: _____

Red:

Easy Stroganoff with Fettuccini and Bean Medley

Our family rating: 8
Your family rating: _____

Blue:

Citrus Chicken (or Pork) with Rice and Broccoli

Our family rating: 9.5
Your family rating: _____

Yellow:

Meatball Souvlaki with Fixings on Pita and Salad

Our family rating: 8.5
Your family rating: _____

Chicken in a Mango Cream Sauce on Pasta with Asparagus

Instructions:

Don't change yet! Take out equipment.

1. Fill a large **stove-top** pot with water and bring to a boil.

2. Heat oil in a large nonstick **fry pan** or wok at med-high. Cut chicken into small bite size pieces and gradually add to pan as you cut. Stir until meat is no longer pink.
   ...meanwhile...
   Slice onion and pepper into thin strips and add to pan as you slice.
   Add garlic, curry paste and flour to pan in that order. Stir to coat chicken.

   Gradually add chicken broth, mango juice and milk, stirring as you add.

   Add peach jam and hot chili flakes.

3. Place pasta in boiling water, stir and cook uncovered. Set timer according to package directions, approx 8 minutes.
   ...meanwhile...

4. Snap off bottom nodes of asparagus and discard. Rinse in colander or steamer basket. Place a small amount of water in the bottom of a **stove-top** pot and bring to a full boil with the asparagus in the basket above. Cover and set timer for 4 minutes...or **microwave** for the same amount of time.
   ...when timer rings for asparagus...
   Drain water. Toss in pot with butter and salt.

   ...when timer rings for pasta...
5. Rinse pasta in colander with hot water and return to cooking pot, **no heat**.
   I like to toss it with a little olive oil and basil.

   If fresh mango is available, I like to toss 1/3 of the mango right in the sauce at the end. I cube the balance and use it for garnish!

Ingredients:

Take out ingredients.
water

1 tsp canola oil
3 chicken breasts, boneless, skinless
 (1 lb or 450 g)

1/2 red onion
1/2 green bell pepper
2 tsp prepared garlic (from a jar)
1 heaping Tbsp curry paste (Madras Indian)
2 Tbsp flour
1/2 cup chicken broth, reduced-sodium
1/2 cup mango/tangerine juice blend
1 cup 1% milk
1 Tbsp peach jam (or mango chutney)
1 tsp hot chili flakes (optional)

3/4 lb or 340 g spaghettini pasta, whole wheat

20 asparagus spears (1 lb or 450 g)

water

1 tsp butter and pinch of salt (optional)

Kids, if you are making this for your parents, this is very gourmet...so have a little fun with it. You don't always have to serve things in a boring way. Be creative. Place the asparagus in a bowl standing up. Dish in the pasta and top with the sauce. Your parents will feel like they are at a specialty restaurant...aaand you know what happy fed parents are like!!!

Serves 4-6

DINNER IS READY IN 25 MINUTES

Equipment List:

Large stove-top pot
Large nonstick fry pan or wok
Stove top pot w/steamer basket
2 cutting boards
Colander
Sharp meat knife
Sharp veggie knife
Stirring spoon
Pasta fork
Can opener
Measuring cups and spoons

Per serving:

Calories	377
Fat	4.8 g
Protein	29.8 g
Carbohydrate	57.0 g
Fiber	2.4 g
Sodium	219 mg

U.S. Food Exchanges:	Cdn. Food Choices:	
2 1/2 Starch	3 1/2	Carb
2 1/2 Meat-very lean	3	Meat/Alt
1 Vegetable	1/2	Other
1/2 Fruit		
1/2 Milk-low fat		

20 to prep

W
E
E
K

6

Fish and Chips with Salad

Instructions:

Don't change yet! Take out equipment.
1. Preheat **oven** to 375° F.

2. Tear lettuce into bite size pieces directly into salad spinner. Rinse, spin dry, then place in salad bowl. Wash, then grate carrot over lettuce. Set aside.

3. Pour buttermilk or egg bath into a bowl.

   Pour breadcrumbs, Parmesan and spices into a different bowl to make a coating mix.

   Spray a 9"x 13" cake pan with cooking spray.

   Cut fish into serving pieces approx 3" x 4". Dunk fish into buttermilk, then coating mix and place on sprayed pan.
   Spray the top of each piece of fish with cooking spray.
   Place in **preheated oven** on lower central rack. Set timer for 15 minutes.

4. Spray a different cookie sheet with cooking spray. Place fries on cookie sheet in a single layer. Spray tops of fries and lightly sprinkle with seasoning salt.

   ...when timer rings for fish...
5. Move fish to upper center rack and place fries on bottom center rack. Set timer for 5 minutes.
   ...when timer rings again...
   Toss fries and switch racks with fish again. Set timer for an additional 5 minutes.

   ...when final timer rings...
5. Toss salad with dressing and croutons.

Ingredients:

Take out ingredients.

1 head green leaf lettuce
2 carrots

1 cup buttermilk (or 2 eggs and 3/4 cup milk combined to make egg bath)
1 cup breadcrumbs
1/4 cup Parmesan cheese, light, grated
1 Tbsp dried parsley
1/4 tsp pepper
1 tsp spicy seasoning blend, salt-free
cooking spray

1 1/2 lb or 680 g firm white fish
  (e.g. cod, halibut or haddock)

cooking spray

cooking spray
1 lb or 450 g frozen 5 minute fries
  I like McCain.
1/2 tsp seasoning salt (optional)

I really like this fish with tartar sauce.
  (recipe on back flap)

I prefer my fries crispy so cook 5 minute fries for 10 minutes.

1/3 cup salad dressing, fat-free
croutons (optional)

Serves 4-6

DINNER IS READY IN 45 MINUTES

Equipment List:

2 cookie sheets w/sides
Salad spinner
Salad bowl
Salad tongs
Cutting board
Cheese grater
2 small mixing bowls
Fork
Sharp meat knife
Vegetable peeler
Measuring cups and spoons

Per serving:

Calories	355
Fat	8.1 g
Protein	28.7 g
Carbohydrate	41.9 g
Fiber	4.6 g
Sodium	513 mg

U.S. Food Exchanges:		Cdn. Food Choices:	
2	Starch	2 1/2	Carb
3 1/2	Meat-lean	4	Meat/Alt
2	Vegetable		

15 to prep

Easy Stroganoff
with Fettuccini and Bean Medley

Instructions:

Don't change yet! Take out equipment.

1. Fill a large **stove-top** pot with water and bring to a boil.

2. Brown meat in a large nonstick **fry-pan** or wok at med-high.
   ...while meat is browning...
   Dice onion, adding to pan as you cut.
   Add spices, chili paste and garlic.

   Wash and slice mushrooms adding to pan as you slice. Add red wine and brown sugar, then boil down for about 5 minutes.
   Add chicken broth, dill and Worcestershire sauce.

   Reduce heat to med-low and let simmer uncovered. You want it to boil gently to reduce the sauce. *The reason reductions taste so great is because the flavors become more concentrated as the liquid is reduced.*

3. Place pasta in boiling water, stir and cook uncovered. Set timer according to package directions, approx 11 minutes.

4. Melt butter in another nonstick **fry pan** at med-high. Add beans, lemon pepper and soy sauce. Toss to coat, then **reduce heat** to med-low. Stir often, until beans are hot and tender.

   ...when timer rings for pasta...

5. Rinse the pasta under hot water in a colander and let drain. Add pasta to meat pan. Add sour cream. Fold pasta and sour cream into meat mixture.

Ingredients:

Take out ingredients.

water

1 lb or 450 g ground beef, extra-lean

1 onion
1 tsp table blend seasoning, salt-free
1/4 tsp pepper
1/2 tsp Sambal Oelek (crushed chili paste)
 (add more if you like it hot)
 1 Tbsp prepared garlic (from a jar)

10 mushrooms
1/2 cup red wine
1 Tbsp brown sugar
2 cups chicken broth, reduced-sodium
1 Tbsp dry dill weed
2 tsp Worcestershire sauce

3/4 lb or 340 g fettuccini pasta

Chef Style Green Beans
1 tsp butter
1 lb or 450 g green or yellow frozen whole
 beans *I like to blend both types together.*
1/2 tsp lemon pepper, salt-free
1 tsp soy sauce, reduced-sodium

1 cup sour cream, no-fat

Serves 4-6

DINNER IS READY IN 30 MINUTES

Equipment List:

Large stove-top pot
2 large nonstick fry pans or
  woks
Colander
Cutting board
Stirring spoon
Sharp veggie knife
Can opener
Measuring cups and spoons

Per serving:

Calories	460
Fat	10.3 g
Protein	27.0 g
Carbohydrate	62.0 g
Fiber	4.3 g
Sodium	318 mg

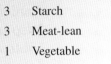

U.S. Food Exchanges:		Cdn. Food Choices:	
3	Starch	4	Carb
3	Meat-lean	4	Meat/Alt
1	Vegetable		
1/2	Milk-fat free		

W
E
E
K

6

Citrus Chicken (or Pork)
with Rice and Broccoli

Instructions:

...the night before...
Take out equipment.

1. Unravel thighs, then flatten and scrunch together in an oven-safe baking dish or pan.

   Combine the following in a small bowl: honey-garlic sauce, orange juice, red wine, brown sugar, spices and garlic.

   Pour sauce evenly over chicken.
   Flip the chicken around with a fork until each piece is thoroughly coated.
   Cover with plastic wrap and leave in the **fridge** overnight.

   ...when you arrive home...
2. Preheat **oven** to 350° F.

3. Combine rice and water in a large oven-safe pot. Stir, cover and place on center rack of **preheated oven**.

4. Place chicken, uncovered, in **oven** beside rice. Set timer for 55 minutes.

   ...just before chicken is ready...
5. Rinse broccoli in colander or steamer basket. Place a small amount of water in the bottom of a **stove-top** pot and bring to a full boil with the broccoli in the basket above. Cover and set timer for 3 minutes. ...or microwave at high for 3 minutes.
   Toss with butter if you must.

Ingredients:

Take out ingredients.

chicken thighs, boneless, skinless (1 3/4 lb or 800 g)

1/2 cup honey-garlic sauce
  VH is my favorite
1/2 cup orange juice, unsweetened
1/4 cup red wine
1 1/2 tsp brown sugar
2 tsp ginger powder
1/4 tsp pepper
1 tsp spicy seasoning blend, salt-free
3 tsp prepared garlic (from a jar)
plastic wrap

1 1/2 cups basmati or white rice
3 cups water

1 lb or 450 g broccoli florets
water

butter *(optional)*

Use the left over sauce for drizzling on your rice!!!

Serves 4-6

DINNER IS READY IN 60 MINUTES

Equipment List:

...the night before...

Large lasagna or cake pan
Small mixing bowl
Stirring spoon
Fork
Measuring cups and spoons
Plastic wrap

...when you get home...

Large oven-safe pot w/lid
Stove top pot w/steamer basket
Colander
Measuring cups

Per serving:

Calories	417
Fat	6.1 g
Protein	31.5 g
Carbohydrate	56.6 g
Fiber	1.2 g
Sodium	247 mg

U.S. Food Exchanges:		Cdn. Food Choices:	
3	Starch	3 1/2	Carb
3 1/2	Meat-very lean	5	Meat/Alt
2	Vegetable	1/2	Other

20 to prep

WEEK 6

Meatball Souvlaki with Fixings on Pita

Instructions:

Don't change yet! Take out equipment.

1. Preheat **oven** to 400° F.

2. Mix together, in a large bowl, in this order; beef, egg, bread crumbs, mustard and spice.

    Roll into meatballs (approx 20) and place on broiler pan sprayed with cooking spray. Place in **preheated oven**. Set timer for 15 minutes.

    ...meanwhile...
3. Grate cucumber..
    Combine cucumber, sour cream, crushed garlic and spices in a small bowl.
    Blend together to create tzatziki dip.

    Refrigerate until ready to serve.

    ...when timer rings for meatballs...
4. **Turn oven off** and cover with foil.

5. Place pita, wrapped in foil, on another rack in **oven** until ready to serve.

6. Tear lettuce into bite-size pieces directly into salad spinner. Rinse and spin dry.
    Wash and cut tomatoes into small chunks.
    Sliver onion.

    Serve meatballs in pita bread with tzatziki dip and toppings.

Ingredients:

Take out ingredients

1 lb or 450 g ground beef, extra lean
1 egg
1/4 cup bread crumbs
1 Tbsp Dijon mustard
1/2 tsp Italian seasoning
1/4 tsp pepper
1/8 tsp salt

cooking spray

Tzatziki
1/2 cup English cucumber (unpeeled)
1 cup sour cream, no-fat or light
1-2 cloves garlic
1/2 tsp dry dill weed
1/8 tsp salt
1/8 tsp pepper

aluminum foil

6-8 pita bread

Toppings
1 head green leaf lettuce

2 Roma tomatoes
1/2 red onion

Feta cheese as a topping is such a nice touch. (optional)

Serves 4-6

DINNER IS READY IN 25 MINUTES

Equipment List:

Broiler pan
Large mixing bowl
Small mixing bowl
Cutting board
Sharp veggie knife
Salad spinner
Salad bowl
Salad tongs
Grater
Measuring cups and spoons
Aluminum foil

Per serving:

Calories	351
Fat	6.3 g
Protein	25.2 g
Carbohydrate	47.3 g
Fiber	2.9 g
Sodium	575 mg

U.S. Food Exchanges:		Cdn. Food Choices:	
3	Starch	3	Carb
3	Meat-very lean	4	Meat/Alt

20
to
prep

WEEK 6

Week 7 is a Survival Week!

A survival week is the easiest approach that a person can take to ensure they don't end up in the drive through lane or make dinner from a box!

You know, it's one of those weeks when you can't even imagine thinking about dinner! If you're a single student, it may be exam week. If you're a single exec, it may be getting the draft of a presentation ready. If you have a family, it may be Christmas concert week. Yuck!!!! I know the kids look adorable, but that week is sheer…well you know, the opposite of heaven. Presents for the teachers, the friends, the mystery gift, the plays, the concerts, the plays, the concerts, the plays, the concerts! If you're any of the above, if you're human, you know the kind of week I mean! I've touched on some of these ideas in the section "Make ahead while you're already cooking" as well.

As the shopper, cook, and provider, there is so much guilt attached to how we are feeding ourselves and our families. I wanted to create a survival week for two reasons.

First, I want you to know that our family isn't perfect. You should see my laundry room right now! You would have loved the very heated discussion I had with my family last night which was immediately followed by children filing out to the driveway 2 by 2 to haul their garbage out of the very large garbage bag, A.K.A. the family vehicle!

Second, I want to give you a guideline of how you can do some of these simple things with recipes you have and use regularly. Is there a sauce that can be brewing while you're unloading groceries? Is there a marinade you love that you can throw on the steaks or chicken pieces to ensure a great stir-fry? I want to put a bug in your ear, a fire under your butt, to create at least 2 of these "Survival Weeks" on your own. If you have two survival weeks, you have the ability to get through the worst of weeks without eating artery-clogging, energy-draining food. This is a good thing!

Don't spend your weekend cooking for the week, unless it's something you love to do.

Instead...

- Brown ground meats ahead and freeze them in bags while unloading groceries.

- Marinate and portion meat in the freezer for easy stir-fries.

- Keep fresh noodles on hand, such as Shanghai or Singapore noodles, cut up a few veggies, drizzle with stir-fry sauce and voila, an instant back up plan.

- Purchase a pre-roasted chicken from the deli. It's easy to boil a few potatoes or make up a pot of rice and stir-fry some veggies as a side dish when you know the main course is done.

Week 7 Do-ahead Preparation, While Unpacking Your Groceries

Instructions:

1. **Cajun Peppered Steak**   Yellow
Poke steak all over with a fork. Sprinkle with spice. Place in freezer bag and toss in **freezer**. You can prepare the sesame sauce from pg 150 now or anytime before the meal.

2. **Honey BBQ Roaster Chicken**   Red
Slice chicken in half with a large knife. Place flat side down (both halves) on a microwave-safe pan. Combine honey-garlic sauce with ketchup in a small bowl. Blend together and brush all over chicken. Sprinkle with spice. Cover and place in **freezer**.

3. **Lazy Leftover Lasagna**   Green
Spread a small amount of pasta sauce on the bottom of a lasagna pan. Remove all veggies you like from the fridge that are considered a leftover...*that aren't moldy.* Separate equal amounts of each into 3 parts.

   Layer in this order; 1/3 uncooked lasagna noodles, 1/3 leftover ingredients, 1/3 broccoli, and 1/3 sauce. Sprinkle with 1/3 Parmesan and 1/2 cup grated mozzarella cheese.

   Repeat two more times; however, on final layer do not add the mozzarella cheese at the end. Pour 1/2 cup 1% milk all over. Cover tightly with foil shiny side down and **freeze**.

4. **Honey-Garlic Chicken Burgers**   Yellow
Remove chicken breasts from package and place in freezer bag. Pour honey-garlic sauce over top. Seal and squish sauce all over the chicken. Toss in **freezer**.

5. **Teriyaki Beef Stir-Fry**   Red
Slice beef into thin strips against the grain. Place in freezer bag. Pour honey-garlic sauce and ginger into bag. Seal bag, squish sauce all over to coat. Toss in **freezer**.

Ingredients:

Our Family Rating: 9
1 1/2 lbs or 675 g lean sirloin steak
2 tsp peppercorn seasoning, salt-free
1 tsp garlic powder
1 lge zipper lock freezer bag

Our Family Rating: 8
1 pre-roasted chicken from the deli
** (2 lbs or 900 g)**
1/2 cup honey-garlic sauce
1/2 cup ketchup
1 tsp spicy seasoning blend, salt-free
plastic wrap

Our Family Rating: 9
2 cans tomato pasta sauce
** (24 fl oz or 680 mL each)**
  (choose a lower-sodium brand)
leftover veggies in fridge (2-3 cups of
  chopped onions, celery, peppers, etc.)

12 (uncooked) lasagna noodles
** (10 oz or 285 g)**
3/4 lb or 340 g broccoli florets (4 cups)
1/2 cup Parmesan cheese, light, grated
1 1/2 cups mozzarella cheese, part-skim,
shredded (set 1/2 cup aside in fridge for final
layer on day you are cooking the lasagna)

1/2 cup 1% milk (or soy milk)
aluminum foil

Our Family Rating: 10
4 chicken breasts, boneless, skinless
** (1 1/2 lbs or 675 g)**
1 large zipper lock freezer bag
1/2 cup honey-garlic sauce

Our Family Rating: 9.5
1 1/2 lbs or 675 g lean sirloin or flank
1/2 cup honey-garlic sauce
1 tsp ginger powder
1 large zipper lock freezer bag

Cajun Peppered Steak with Baby Potatoes and Mixed Beans

Instructions:

See prep ahead on page 149.
Remember to defrost frozen steak.
Don't change yet! Take out equipment.

1. Wash potatoes and place in a large **stove-top** pot with cold water. Bring to a boil at high heat then **reduce heat** to a low boil. Set timer for 15 minutes or until you can slide a knife into the potato easily.

   ...meanwhile...

2. Prepare sesame steak sauce by combining the following ingredients in a small bowl; tahini, spices, garlic, soy sauce, mayonnaise and water. Blend really well with a whisk or a fork to combine until smooth.
   It looks disgusting but tastes amazing.

3. Rinse beans in colander.
   Heat butter in a large fry pan or wok at med.
   Add beans, lemon pepper and soy sauce.
   Toss to coat, then **reduce heat** to med-low.
   Cook until beans are hot and tender. Stir often.

4. **Grill** seasoned steak on the **BBQ** or **broil** in the oven depending on the season.

   To broil a steak nicely in the oven, spray the broiler pan with cooking spray first. Watch the steak carefully until you see the one side get a little crusty. Turn it over and do the same to the other side. This gives you a nicely seared med steak. I broiled the steak in the picture...and remember I don't use photography tricks, so this really is what the steak should look like.

Ingredients:

If you didn't prep ahead you can still make the entire meal just before dinner.
Take out ingredients.

20 baby potatoes (or cut 4 large)
water

Sesame Steak Sauce
1/4 cup tahini
1/4 tsp ginger powder
1/4 tsp salt
1/8 tsp paprika
1 tsp prepared garlic (from a jar)
2 Tbsp soy sauce, reduced-sodium
1 Tbsp mayonnaise, light
3 Tbsp water

1 lb or 450 g mixed frozen beans
  (or use all green)
1 tsp butter
1/2 tsp lemon pepper seasoning, salt-free
1 tsp soy sauce, reduced-sodum

1 1/2 lbs or 675 g lean sirloin steak
  Seasoned from prep ahead on page 149.

Don't over boil your potatoes; you reduce the starch when they are cooked firm...also note baby potatoes naturally have a lower glycemic index.

Serves 4-6

About This Meal: *I'm warning you...this sesame steak sauce becomes very addicting. If papaya is available in your area squeeze a little juice onto the steak before you spice and freeze. Papaya is a natural tenderizer and it does magic to a leaner cut of steak! Remember, the leaner the cut, the less tender it will be. This is a great way to get the best of both worlds.*

DINNER IS READY IN 30 MINUTES

Equipment List:

...the prep-ahead day...
Fork
Large zipper lock freezer bag
Measuring spoons

...the eating day...
Large stove-top pot
Large fry pan or wok
BBQ grill or broiler pan
Small mixing bowl
Colander
Large stirring spoon
Fork or whisk
Knife
Measuring cups and spoons

Per serving:

Calories	354
Fat	12.1 g
Protein	27.0 g
Carbohydrate	36.3 g
Fiber	6.5 g
Sodium	419 mg

U.S. Food Exchanges:		Cdn. Food Choices:	
2	Starch	2	Carb
3	Meat-lean	4	Meat/Alt
1	Fat		

Honey BBQ Roaster Chicken
with Citrus Spinach Salad

Instructions:

See prep ahead on page 149.
Remember to defrost frozen chicken.
Don't change yet! Take out equipment.

1. Rinse spinach in basket of salad spinner.
   Spin dry.
   Sliver red onion.
   Wash and slice strawberries.
   Peel mandarins and separate segments.

   Divide spinach on serving plates and top with
   onion, strawberries and mandarin segments.

2. **Microwave** (defrosted) pre-basted cooked
   chicken at medium heat. Set timer for 5 min.
   *You may have to reheat a little more depending
   on your microwave.*

3. Combine mayonnaise, yogurt and poppy seeds
   in a small bowl. Blend using a whisk or fork.
   Set aside on table.

4. Serve with buns.

   ...when timer rings for chicken...
   Dinner is ready.

Ingredients:

**If you didn't prep ahead you can still make
the entire meal just before dinner.**
Take out ingredients.

12 oz or 340 g baby spinach

1/5 of a red onion
6 strawberries
1-2 mandarin oranges

*I love to sprinkle on the candied almond
and pecan salad topping.*
See back flap for recipe. (optional)

1 whole pre-cooked roaster chicken
   (assumes 1 lb or 450 g of actual meat)
   Basted from prep ahead on page 149.

<u>**Poppy Seed Salad Dressing**</u>
1/4 cup mayonnaise, light
1/4 cup French vanilla yogurt, low-fat
1/4 tsp poppy seeds
*You may want to whisk in a tiny bit of 1%
milk if you like your dressing a little runnier.*

4-6 buns, whole wheat or multigrain
butter (optional)

<u>**Serves 4-6**</u>

About This Meal: *This is a crazy, easy, make-ahead meal that literally takes no time at all to what
I call "bank a meal". I love to serve anything citrus on a spinach salad because the iron in spinach
is absorbed better if you combine citrus fruit with it. It also tastes amazing!*

DINNER IS READY IN 25 MINUTES

Equipment List:

...the prep-ahead day...
Microwave-safe pan
Sharp meat knife
Cutting board
Small bowl
Stirring spoon
Spatula or brush
Measuring cups and spoons
Plastic wrap
...the eating day...
Salad spinner and Salad tongs
Small mixing bowl
Cutting board
Whisk or fork
Sharp veggie knife
Measuring cups and spoons

Per serving:

Calories	363
Fat	10.9 g
Protein	27.2 g
Carbohydrate	40.8 g
Fiber	4.2 g
Sodium	668 mg

U.S. Food Exchanges:		Cdn. Food Choices:	
1	Starch	2	Carb
3 1/2	Meat-lean	4	Meat/Alt
1/2	Fruit	1/2	Other
1/2	Fat		
1/2	Other Carb		

10 to prep

Lazy Leftover Lasagna

Instructions:

See prep ahead on page 149.
Remember to defrost frozen lasagna.
Don't change yet! Take out equipment.

1. Preheat **oven** to 450° F.
   Place (defrosted) lasagna in **preheated oven**.
   Set timer for 15 minutes.

   ...when timer rings...
   Reduce heat to 350° F and reset timer for 40 minutes.

   ...when timer rings again...
   Remove foil from top of lasagna pan.
   Sprinkle top with mozzarella cheese.
   Set oven to **broil**. Watch carefully.

   Remove lasagna when cheese has bubbled completely. Let stand about 5 minutes while setting the table.

   If you are really starting to like having this lasagna because there is no prepping on eating day...I suggest you read the section "Make ahead while you're already cooking." You won't believe the stress you can save yourself!!!

Ingredients:

If you didn't prep ahead you can still make the entire meal just before dinner.
Take out ingredients.

Lasagna from prep ahead on page 149.

1/2 cup mozzarella cheese, part-skim, shredded (set aside from prep day)

This is a great stand alone meal that's packed with nutrition, calcium and even veggies. If you have leftover cold veggies from the week, they're a great addition as a side dish.

Serves 6-8

About This Meal: *Let's say you have no leftovers. That happens in my house quite frequently now that our college student has come to realize that it's way cheaper to steal leftovers from home than it is to spend her hard earned cash on food. Make it with just the broccoli. It's amazing!!!*

Remember, one of the best tips with lasagna of any kind is not to put the cheese on the top until it's all cooked. Then take off the foil, put the cheese on the top and broil it until it bubbles. This not only tastes better, but you also don't have the chore of peeling cheese off the top of the foil. This is vegetarian unless you choose to add leftover meats.

DINNER IS READY IN 60 MINUTES

Equipment List:

...the prep-ahead day...
Large lasagna or cake pan
Cutting board
Cheese grater
Sharp veggie knife
Small spatula or spoon
Measuring cups
Aluminum foil

...the eating day...
Cheese grater
Measuring cups

Per serving:

Calories	343
Fat	7.5 g
Protein	17.9 g
Carbohydrate	49.7 g
Fiber	5.6 g
Sodium	764 mg

U.S. Food Exchanges:		Cdn. Food Choices:	
2	Starch	3	Carb
1 1/2	Meat-lean	3	Meat/Alt
2	Vegetable		
1	Fat		
1/2	Milk-low fat		

Honey-Garlic Chicken Burgers with Veggies and Dip

Instructions:

See prep ahead on page 149.
Remember to defrost frozen chicken.
Don't change yet! Take out equipment.

1. Grill chicken breasts on **BBQ** or **broil** in oven until juices run clear and center is no longer pink. (Inside temp should be 160° F.)
   If you spray a little cooking spray directly on lean cuts of meat, it helps them not stick to either the pan or grill.

2. Blend together in a small bowl mayonnaise, sour cream, and spice to make veggie dip. Store in **fridge**.

   Rinse veggies in a colander. Let drip dry.

   Slice red pepper into strips, if you love red peppers.

3. Slice buns and get fixings ready. (e.g. mayonnaise, lettuce, tomato, things you would normally enjoy on a chicken burger)

   That's it! The family will think they're eating junk food and you can make this quicker than if you ordered in!!!

Ingredients:

If you didn't prep ahead you can still make the entire meal just before dinner.
Take out ingredients.

4 marinated chicken breasts
  Marinated from prep ahead on page 149.

cooking spray (optional)

Veggie Dip
1/4 cup mayonnaise, light
1/4 cup sour cream, no-fat
1/2 tsp garlic & herb seasoning, salt-free

1/2 lb or 225 g baby carrots
1/2 lb or 225 g broccoli and cauliflower
  (cut and packaged from produce aisle)
1 red bell pepper (optional)

6-8 whole wheat or multigrain buns
fixings of your choice (optional)

<u>**Serves 4-6**</u>

About This Meal: *This is the junk food meal of the week. But you would never know it with the nutritional data. Whether I'm making all of this week's meals or not, I sometimes throw these chicken breasts into a freezer bag after buying groceries on other weeks. They always provide me with that emergency kids-will-love-me meal in a pinch!*
I also love to make up veggie burgers with a big marinated portabella mushroom and a slice of grilled or pan fried zucchini and onions. Sprinkle on some grated Parmesan and it's a mouth watering experience.

DINNER IS READY IN 30 MINUTES

Equipment List:

...the prep-ahead day...
Measuring cups
Large zipper lock freezer bag

...the eating day...
BBQ grill or broiler pan
BBQ tongs or flipper
Small mixing bowl
Colander
Cutting board
Bread knife
Sharp veggie knife
Spoon
Measuring cups and spoons

Per serving:

Calories	359
Fat	7.0 g
Protein	31.7 g
Carbohydrate	42.9 g
Fiber	4.4 g
Sodium	518 mg

U.S. Food Exchanges:		Cdn. Food Choices:	
2	Starch	2	Carb
3 1/2	Meat-very lean	4 1/2	Meat/Alt
2	Vegetable	1/2	Other

Teriyaki Beef (or Chicken) Stir Fry on Rice

Instructions:

See prep ahead on page 149.
Remember to defrost frozen beef.
Don't change yet! Take out equipment.

1. Combine rice and water in a large microwave-safe pot with lid. **Microwave** at high 10 minutes, then medium 10 minutes.

2. Heat oil in a large nonstick **fry pan** or wok at high heat.
   Add (defrosted) marinated beef to pan. Toss beef until slightly browned, then **reduce heat** to medium.

3. Rinse stir-fry veggies in a colander. Add to pan and toss. Keep tossing stir-fry until veggies are cooked through but still crisp.

   ...when timer rings for rice...
4. Let rice stand for 5 minutes.

   Sprinkle toasted sesame seeds on top of stir-fry if you wish.

Ingredients:

If you didn't prep ahead you can still make the entire meal just before dinner.
Take out ingredients.

1 1/2 cups basmati or white rice
3 cups water

1 tsp sesame oil

marinated beef strips
  Marinated from prep ahead on page 149.

1 lb or 450 g frozen stir-fry mixed vegetables
  (or use a fresh veggie packaged blend and cook a few minutes longer)

toasted sesame seeds (optional)

<u>**Serves 4-6**</u>

About This Meal: *For a ridiculously fast meal, this is amazing. In fact, what a way to keep on top of things all the time!! On other weeks when I have steak on the menu, it's so easy to buy extra, slice it up into strips and marinate it. If I have a package of frozen stir-fry veggies available in the freezer, it's a guarantee that I won't cheat if I forgot to take something out of the freezer in the morning. Vegetarians...lose the meat...just make sure you're getting your protein.*

DINNER IS READY IN 25 MINUTES

Equipment List:

...the prep-ahead day...
Cutting board
Sharp meat knife
Measuring cups and spoons
Large zipper lock freezer bag

...the eating day...
Large microwave-safe pot w/lid
Large nonstick fry pan or wok
Colander
Large stirring spoon
Measuring cups and spoons

Per serving:

Calories	416
Fat	8.4 g
Protein	25.6 g
Carbohydrate	58.6 g
Fiber	4.1 g
Sodium	194 mg

U.S. Food Exchanges:		Cdn. Food Choices:	
3	Starch	4	Carb
3	Meat-lean	4	Meat/Alt
2	Vegetable		

10 to prep

Write your own recipe reading left to right.

Prep Time

_____

Instructions:

Don't change yet! Take out equipment.

Ingredients:

Take out ingredients.

DINNER IS READY IN ____ MINUTES

**A shift in how I did things changed everything.
It gave me back my time, my health and family dinners.**

I call these Eat Sheets™.

What we usually do is write
down only what we need.

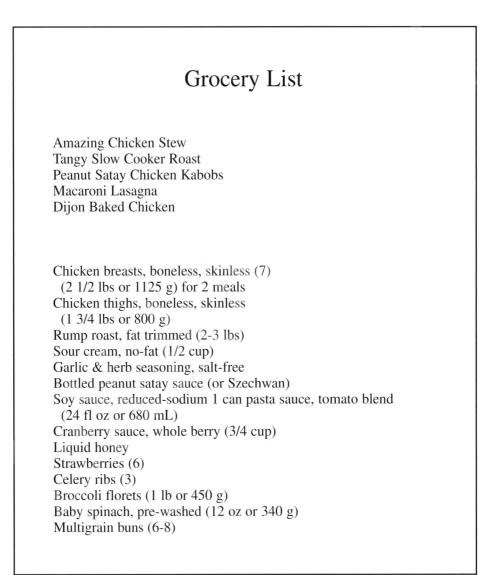

Grocery List

Amazing Chicken Stew
Tangy Slow Cooker Roast
Peanut Satay Chicken Kabobs
Macaroni Lasagna
Dijon Baked Chicken

Chicken breasts, boneless, skinless (7)
  (2 1/2 lbs or 1125 g) for 2 meals
Chicken thighs, boneless, skinless
  (1 3/4 lbs or 800 g)
Rump roast, fat trimmed (2-3 lbs)
Sour cream, no-fat (1/2 cup)
Garlic & herb seasoning, salt-free
Bottled peanut satay sauce (or Szechwan)
Soy sauce, reduced-sodium 1 can pasta sauce, tomato blend
  (24 fl oz or 680 mL)
Cranberry sauce, whole berry (3/4 cup)
Liquid honey
Strawberries (6)
Celery ribs (3)
Broccoli florets (1 lb or 450 g)
Baby spinach, pre-washed (12 oz or 340 g)
Multigrain buns (6-8)

This will only help you buy groceries on the week you make the list.
Your grocery needs will be different on a different week.

Eat Sheet™

RECIPE NAME	Page
Amazing Chicken Stew on Rice	114
Tangy Slow Cooker Roast, Potatoes, Peas	116
Peanut Satay Chicken Kabobs, Spinach Salad	118
Macaroni Lasagna, Veggies & Dip	120
Dijon Baked Chicken, Rice, Broccoli	122

MEATS
Chicken breasts, boneless, skinless (7)
  (2 1/2 lbs or 1125 g) for 2 meals
Chicken thighs, boneless, skinless
  (1 3/4 lbs or 800 g)
Rump roast, fat trimmed (2-3 lbs)
Ground beef, extra-lean (1 lb or 450 g)

DAIRY
Butter (optional)
Sour cream, no-fat (1/2 cup)
Cheddar cheese, light, shredded (2 cups)

PRODUCE
Onion (1)
Baby potatoes (20) or 4 large potatoes
Celery ribs (3)
Broccoli florets (1 lb or 450 g)
Precut veggies (1 1/2 lbs or 675 g)
  (e.g. celery, cauliflower, broccoli and carrots)
Mushrooms (12)
Baby spinach, pre-washed (12 oz or 340 g)
Strawberries (6)

DRY ESSENTIALS
Basmati or white rice (3 cups) for 2 meals
Macaroni, whole wheat (2 1/2 cups)
Croutons (1/2 cup) (optional for Salad)

BAKERY
Multigrain buns (6-8)

SPICES
Curry powder
Garlic & herb seasoning, salt-free
Hot chili flakes (optional)
Italian seasoning
Lemon pepper
Onion flakes
Table blend seasoning, salt-free
Pepper

BAKING GOODS
Cooking spray
Sesame seeds (optional for Chicken Kabobs)
Brown gravy mix, dry

HELPERS
Worcestershire sauce
Soy sauce, reduced-sodium
Bottled peanut satay sauce (or Szechwan)
Sambal Oelek (crushed chili paste)
Dijon mustard
Mayonnaise, light
1 can cream of chicken soup, reduced-sodium
  (10 fl oz or 284 mL)
1 can pasta sauce, tomato blend
  (24 fl oz or 680 mL)
Raspberry vinaigrette, low-fat
Cranberry sauce, whole berry (3/4 cup)
Liquid honey

FROZEN FOODS
Broccoli florets (3/4 lb or 340 g)
Baby carrots (1/2 lb or 225 g)
Baby peas (3 cups)

OTHER
Bamboo skewers (4-6)
Aluminum foil
Plastic wrap
Plastic resealable bag (1 large)

This goes into a plastic sheet protector and can be used to create a grocery list on any given week. Checking for groceries is a great job to delegate.

Eat Sheet™

Create your Eat Sheet™ at www.eatingforward.com
Save it to your computer then print it out anytime.
Cross off the items you don't need to purchase at the grocery store.

Eat Sheet™
Week 4

RECIPE NAME	Page
Amazing Chicken Stew on Rice	114
Tangy Slow Cooker Roast, Potatoes, Peas	116
Peanut Satay Chicken Kabobs, Spinach Salad	118
Macaroni Lasagna, Veggies & Dip	120
Dijon Baked Chicken, Rice, Broccoli	122

MEATS
Chicken breasts, boneless, skinless (7)
 (2 1/2 lbs or 1125 g) for 2 meals
Chicken thighs, boneless, skinless
 (1 3/4 lbs or 800 g)
Rump roast, fat trimmed (2-3 lbs)
~~Ground beef, extra-lean (1 lb or 450 g)~~

DAIRY
~~Butter (optional)~~
Sour cream, no-fat (1/2 cup)
~~Cheddar cheese, light, shredded (2 cups)~~

PRODUCE
~~Onion (1)~~
~~Baby potatoes (20) or 4 large potatoes~~
Celery ribs (3)
Broccoli florets (1 lb or 450 g)
~~Precut veggies (1 1/2 lbs or 675 g)~~
~~(e.g. celery, cauliflower, broccoli and carrots)~~
~~Mushrooms (12)~~
Baby spinach, pre-washed (12 oz or 340 g)
Strawberries (6)

DRY ESSENTIALS
~~Basmati or white rice (3 cups) for 2 meals~~
~~Macaroni, whole wheat (2 1/2 cups)~~
~~Croutons (1/2 cup) (optional for Salad)~~

BAKERY
Multigrain buns (6-8)

SPICES
~~Curry powder~~
Garlic & herb seasoning, salt-free
~~Hot chili flakes (optional)~~
~~Italian seasoning~~
~~Lemon pepper~~
~~Onion flakes~~
~~Table blend seasoning, salt-free~~
~~Pepper~~

BAKING GOODS
~~Cooking spray~~
~~Sesame seeds (optional for Chicken Kabobs)~~
~~Brown gravy mix, dry~~

HELPERS
~~Worcestershire sauce~~
Soy sauce, reduced-sodium
Bottled peanut satay sauce (or Szechwan)
~~Sambal Oelek (crushed chili paste)~~
~~Dijon mustard~~
~~Mayonnaise, light~~
~~1 can cream of chicken soup, reduced-sodium~~
~~(10 fl oz or 284 mL)~~
~~1 can pasta sauce, tomato blend~~
~~(24 fl oz or 680 mL)~~
~~Raspberry vinaigrette, low-fat~~
Cranberry sauce, whole berry (3/4 cup)
Liquid honey

FROZEN FOODS
~~Broccoli florets (3/4 lb or 340 g)~~
~~Baby carrots (1/2 lb or 225 g)~~
~~Baby peas (3 cups)~~

OTHER
~~Bamboo skewers (4-6)~~
~~Aluminum foil~~
~~Plastic wrap~~
~~Plastic resealable bag (1 large)~~

164

MEATS

Chicken breasts, boneless, skinless (4)
  (1 1/2 lbs or 675 g)
Chicken thighs, boneless, skinless
  (1 3/4 lb or 800 g)
Ground turkey (1 lb or 450 g)
Flank or sirloin steak (1 lb or 450 g)
Ground beef, extra-lean (1 1/2 lbs or 675 g)

DAIRY

Butter
French vanilla yogurt, low-fat
Milk, 1% milk fat
Sour cream, no-fat (1/4 cup)
Cottage cheese, 1% (8 oz or 250 g)
Mozzarella cheese, part-skim, shredded (1 cup)
Parmesan cheese, light, grated

PRODUCE

Baby potatoes (20) or 4 large potatoes
Fresh garlic (from a jar)
Onion (1/2)
Green onions (2)
Celery ribs (4) for 2 meals
Baby carrots (1 1/4 lbs or 575 g) for 2 meals
Red bell pepper (1) for 2 meals
Yellow bell pepper (1 small)
Cucumber (1)
Baby spinach, prewashed (12 oz or 350 g)
Broccoli florets (1 1/2 lbs or 675 g) for 2 meals
Fixings of your choice (for Chicken Burgers)
Oranges (2)

DRY ESSENTIALS

Corn flake crumbs
Basmati or white rice (3 cups) for 2 meals
Manicotti noodles (8 oz or 250 g)

OTHER

Red wine (can be non-alcoholic)
Aluminum foil
Freezer bag, resealable (1 large)

SPICES

Curry powder
Ginger powder (or prepared ginger from a jar)
Garlic & herb seasoning, salt-free
Garlic powder
Italian seasoning
Mrs. Dash Original seasoning
Onion powder
Poppy seeds
Pepper
Red crushed chili flakes (optional)
Table blend seasoning, salt-free

BAKING GOODS

Cooking spray
Olive oil, extra-virgin
Sesame oil
Balsamic vinegar
Sugar
Brown sugar
Cornstarch

HELPERS

Orange juice, unsweetened (1/2 cup)
Liquid honey
Applesauce, unsweetened
1 can chicken broth, reduced-sodium
  (10 oz or 284 mL)
1 can cream of mushroom soup (10 oz or 284 mL)
1 can tomato soup (10 oz or 284 mL)
Tomato pasta sauce, choose a lower sodium brand
  (24 fl oz or 680 mL)
Salsa
Dijon mustard
Ketchup
Mayonnaise, light
Worcestershire sauce
Soy sauce, reduced-sodium
Oyster sauce
Thai peanut sauce (can be Szechuan
  or peanut satay)
Sambal Oelek (crushed chili paste)

FROZEN FOOD

Snow peas (1 1/3 lbs or 600 g) or use fresh

BAKERY

Hamburger buns, whole wheat 6-8

Custom Eat Sheet™

RECIPE NAME   Page

_____

_____

_____

_____

_____

MEATS

DAIRY

PRODUCE

DRY ESSENTIALS

SPICES

BAKING GOODS

HELPERS

FROZEN FOODS

BAKERY

OTHER

RECIPE NAME	Page
Hot Beef & Pasta on Caesar Salad	90
Maple Cranberry Chicken, Rice, Broccoli	92
Curried Salmon & Egg Noodle Bake, Peas	94
Savory Pot Roast, Harvest Veggies	96
Thai Chicken Pizza, Veggie Toss	98

MEATS

Flank steak (1 lb or 450 g) (or use chicken)

Sirloin or round roast, boneless, trimmed
   (2-3 lbs or 900-1350 g)

Chicken breasts, boneless, skinless (5)
   (1 3/4 lbs or 825 g) for 2 meals

Salmon, cooked, boneless, skinless (3/4 cup)
   (canned or fresh)

DAIRY

Milk, 1% milk fat

Butter

Cheddar cheese, light, shredded (3/4 cup) or more

Mozzarella cheese, part-skim, shredded (1 cup)

PRODUCE

Gourmet Caesar salad dressing, light (3 Tbsp)

Fresh garlic (from a jar)

Onion (1/2)

Green onions (6) for 2 meals

Baby potatoes (20) or 4 large potatoes

Baby carrots (1 lb or 450 g) or 4 large carrots

Red bell pepper (1/2)

Yellow bell pepper (1/2)

Broccoli florets (1 1/2 lb or 675 g) for 2 meals

Veggie mixture, cut (1 lb or 450 g)
   (e.g. carrots, cauliflower, broccoli, celery)

Mushrooms (21) for 3 recipes

Bean sprouts (1 cup)

Leaf lettuce (1 head)

DRY ESSENTIALS

Egg noodles, broad (3/4 lb or 340 g)

Spiral pasta, whole wheat (2 cups)

Basmati or white rice (1 1/4 cups)

SPICES

Cayenne (optional)

Curry powder

Garlic & herb seasoning, salt-free

Ginger powder

Hot chili flakes (optional)

Mrs. Dash Original seasoning

Onion flakes

Rosemary leaves

Table blend seasoning, salt free

Salt & Pepper

BAKING GOODS

Cooking spray

Olive oil, extra-virgin

Sesame oil

Balsamic vinegar

Apple cider vinegar

Dry brown gravy mix

Flour

Maple syrup

Cranberries, dried, unsweetened

HELPERS

Peanut butter, light

Vegetable juice (1/4 cup)

1 can beef broth, reduced-sodium
   (10 fl oz or 284 mL)

1 can cream of asparagus soup
   (10 fl oz or 284 mL)

Teriyaki sauce, reduced-sodium

Soy sauce, reduced-sodium

Mayonnaise, light

FROZEN FOODS

Baby peas (3 cups)

BAKERY

Pizza Crust, 12" (1/2 lb or 225 g) pre-made

OTHER

Paper towel

Aluminum foil

Custom Eat Sheet™

RECIPE NAME   Page

_____

_____

_____

_____

_____

MEATS

DAIRY

PRODUCE

DRY ESSENTIALS

SPICES

BAKING GOODS

HELPERS

FROZEN FOODS

BAKERY

OTHER

RECIPE NAME

MEATS

Chicken, pre-roasted from the deli (2 lbs or 900 g)
Chicken thighs, boneless, skinless
  (1 3/4 lbs or 800 g)
Ground beef, extra-lean (1 lb or 450 g)
Lean sirloin or flank steak (1 1/2 lbs or 675 g)
Scallops, fresh or frozen (1/2 lb or 225 g)

DAIRY

Milk, 1% milk fat
Butter
Cheddar cheese, light, shredded (2 cups) or more
Vanilla yogurt, low-fat (1/2 cup)

PRODUCE

Fresh garlic (from a jar)
Onion (1)
Red Onion (1/2)
Carrots (3)
Potatoes (4 large)
Celery ribs (4)
Red bell pepper (1/2)
Yellow bell pepper (1/2)
Broccoli florets (1 1/2 lbs or 675 g)
Green leaf lettuce (1 head)
Assorted veggies (1/4 lb or 125 g) (can use
  leftover veggies e.g. tomatoes, peppers)
Seasonal fruit, chopped (2 cups) (e.g. oranges,
  grapes, cantaloupe)

DRY ESSENTIALS

Basmati rice or white rice (1 1/2 cups)
Egg noodles, broad (3/4 lb or 340 g)
Penne pasta, whole wheat (3/4 lb or 340 g)

SPICES

Basil leaves (optional for Penne Pasta)
Garlic & herb seasoning, salt-free
Hot chili flakes (optional)
Mrs. Dash Original seasoning
Onion flakes
Paprika
Table blend seasoning, salt-free
Pepper

BAKING GOODS

Cooking spray
Olive oil, extra-virgin
Flour

HELPERS

1 can of crab or lobster meat (6 oz or 170 g)
Chicken broth, reduced-sodium (64 fl oz or 2 litres)
  (for Seafood Chowder)
1 can cream of chicken soup, reduced-sodium
  (10 fl oz or 284 mL)
1 can beef consommé (10 fl oz or 284 mL)
1 can Italian stewed tomatoes (14 fl oz or 398 mL)
Ketchup
Prepared mustard
Worcestershire sauce
Salad dressing, favorite, light
Catalina salad dressing, low-fat
1 can fruit salad, unsweetened (1 3/4 cups)
Whole cranberry sauce (3/4 cup)

FROZEN FOODS

Baby peas (3 cups)
Baby carrots (1 lb or 450 g)

BAKERY

Hamburger buns, whole wheat (4-6)
Multigrain bread (optional with Seafood Chowder)

OTHER

Aluminum foil

Custom Eat Sheet™

RECIPE NAME   Page

_____

_____

_____

_____

_____

MEATS

DAIRY

PRODUCE

DRY ESSENTIALS

SPICES

BAKING GOODS

HELPERS

FROZEN FOODS

BAKERY

OTHER

MEATS

Chicken breasts, boneless, skinless (7)
  (2 1/2 lbs or 1125 g) for 2 meals
Chicken thighs, boneless, skinless
  (1 3/4 lbs or 800 g)
Rump roast, fat trimmed (2-3 lbs)
Ground beef, extra-lean (1 lb or 450 g)

DAIRY

Butter (optional)
Sour cream, no-fat (1/2 cup)
Cheddar cheese, light, shredded (2 cups)

PRODUCE

Onion (1)
Baby potatoes (20) or 4 large potatoes
Celery ribs (3)
Broccoli florets (1 lb or 450 g)
Precut veggies (1 1/2 lbs or 675 g)
  (e.g. celery, cauliflower, broccoli and carrots)
Mushrooms (12)
Baby spinach, pre-washed (12 oz or 340 g)
Strawberries (6)

DRY ESSENTIALS

Basmati or white rice (3 cups) for 2 meals
Macaroni, whole wheat (2 1/2 cups)
Croutons (1/2 cup) (optional for Salad)

BAKERY

Multigrain buns (6-8)

SPICES

Curry powder
Garlic & herb seasoning, salt-free
Hot chili flakes (optional)
Italian seasoning
Lemon pepper
Onion flakes
Table blend seasoning, salt-free
Pepper

BAKING GOODS

Cooking spray
Sesame seeds (optional for Chicken Kabobs)
Brown gravy mix, dry

HELPERS

Worcestershire sauce
Soy sauce, reduced-sodium
Bottled peanut satay sauce (or Szechwan)
Sambal Oelek (crushed chili paste)
Dijon mustard
Mayonnaise, light
1 can cream of chicken soup, reduced-sodium
  (10 fl oz or 284 mL)
1 can pasta sauce, tomato blend
  (24 fl oz or 680 mL)
Raspberry vinaigrette, low-fat
Cranberry sauce, whole berry (3/4 cup)
Liquid honey

FROZEN FOODS

Broccoli florets (3/4 lb or 340 g)
Baby carrots (1/2 lb or 225 g)
Baby peas (3 cups)

OTHER

Bamboo skewers (4-6)
Aluminum foil
Plastic wrap
Plastic resealable bag (1 large)

Custom Eat Sheet™

RECIPE NAME   Page

_____

_____

_____

_____

_____

MEATS

DAIRY

PRODUCE

DRY ESSENTIALS

SPICES

BAKING GOODS

HELPERS

FROZEN FOODS

BAKERY

OTHER

RECIPE NAME

MEATS

Chicken, pre-roasted from the deli
  (only half of a 2 lbs or 900 g chicken needed)
  or use 1/2 lb or 225 g deli cooked chicken breast
Chicken breasts, boneless, skinless (3)
  (1 lb or 450 g)
Chicken thighs, boneless, skinless (10-12)
  (1 3/4 lbs or 800 g)
Ground beef, extra-lean (1 1/2 lbs or 675 g)
Salmon filets (pink), boneless, skinless (4)
  (6 oz or 170 g each filet)

DAIRY

Butter
Milk, 1% milk fat
Sour cream, no-fat (1/2 cup)
Parmesan cheese, light, grated
  (optional for Tortellini)

PRODUCE

Cheese tortellini (4 1/2 cups)
Fresh garlic (from a jar)
Onions (2) for 3 meals
Baby potatoes (20) or 4 large potatoes
Carrots (3)
Celery ribs (3) for 2 meals
Green bell pepper (1)
Asparagus spears (20)
Broccoli florets (1 lb or 450 g)
Precut veggies (1 lb or 450 g)
  (e.g. celery, cauliflower, carrots, broccoli)
Mushrooms (5)

DRY ESSENTIALS

Basmati or white rice (2 1/4 cups) for 2 meals
Bird's nest pasta bundles (3/4 lb or 340 g)

OTHER

Paper towel
Medium size paper bag (grocery type)
Aluminum foil (heavy)

SPICES

Cayenne
Chives, dried
Garlic & herb seasoning, salt-free
Garlic powder
Hot chili flakes (optional)
Italian seasoning
Mrs. Dash Original seasoning
Poultry seasoning
Table blend seasoning, salt-free
Salt & Pepper

BAKING GOODS

Cooking spray
Olive oil, extra-virgin
Canola oil
Sesame oil (optional for Bird's Nest pasta)
Vinegar
Cider vinegar
Brown sugar
Flour
Cornstarch
Brown gravy mix, dry
Evaporated milk, low-fat

HELPERS

Chicken broth, reduced-sodium
  (58 fl oz or 1650 mL) for 2 meals
1 can beef broth, reduced-sodium
  (10 fl oz or 284 mL)
1 can tomato sauce, no-salt added
  (14 fl oz or 398 mL)
1 can mushroom soup, reduced-sodium
  (10 fl oz or 284 mL)
Soy sauce, reduced-sodium
Thai peanut sauce
Dijon mustard
Mayonnaise, light
1 can pineapple chunks, unsweetened
  (20 oz or 540 mL)

FROZEN FOODS

Pea pods (10 oz or 300 g)
Baby peas (1 cup)

BAKERY

Multigrain buns (6)

Custom Eat Sheet™

RECIPE NAME   Page

_____

_____

_____

_____

_____

MEATS

DAIRY

PRODUCE

DRY ESSENTIALS

SPICES

BAKING GOODS

HELPERS

FROZEN FOODS

BAKERY

OTHER

RECIPE NAME

MEATS

Chicken breasts, boneless, skinless (3)
  (1 lb or 450 g)
Chicken thighs, boneless, skinless (10-12)
  (1 3/4 lbs or 800 g) can use pork
Ground beef, extra-lean (2 lbs or 900 g) for 2 meals
Firm white fish (e.g. cod, halibut or haddock)
  (1 1/2 lbs or 680 g)

DAIRY

Butter
Milk, 1% milk fat (1 cup)
Buttermilk (1 cup) or use 2 eggs and milk
Sour cream, no-fat or light (2 cups) for 2 meals
Egg (1)
Feta cheese (optional for Meatball Souvlaki)
Parmesan cheese, light, grated (1/4 cup)

PRODUCE

Garlic cloves (1-2)
Fresh garlic (from a jar)
Onion (1)
Red onion (1) for 2 meals
Carrots (2)
Green bell pepper (1/2)
English cucumber (1/2)
Asparagus spears (20)
Green leaf lettuce (2 heads) for 2 meals
Broccoli florets (1 lb or 450 g)
Mushrooms (10)
Roma tomatoes (2)
Mango (optional for Mango Cream Sauce)

DRY ESSENTIALS

Croutons (optional for Salad)
Spaghettini pasta, whole wheat (3/4 lb or 340 g)
Fettuccini pasta (3/4 lb or 340 g)
Basmati or white rice (1 1/2 cups)

SPICES

Dill weed, dry
Ginger powder
Hot chili flakes (optional)
Italian seasoning
Lemon pepper, salt-free
Parsley, dried
Seasoning salt (optional)
Spicy seasoning blend, salt-free
Table blend seasoning, salt-free
Salt & Pepper

BAKING GOODS

Canola oil
Cooking spray
Flour
Brown sugar

HELPERS

Mango/tangerine juice blend (1/2 cup)
  (or use any mango juice blend)
Orange juice, unsweetened (1/2 cup)
Peach jam
Chicken broth, reduced-sodium (2 1/2 cups)
  for 2 meals
Madras curry paste
Sambal Oelek (crushed chili paste)
Honey-garlic sauce (1/2 cup)
Worcestershire sauce
Soy sauce, reduced-sodium
Dijon mustard
Salad dressing, fat-free

FROZEN FOODS

5-minute fries (1 lb or 450 g)
Green or yellow whole beans (1 lb or 450 g)

BAKERY

Breadcrumbs (1 1/4 cups) for 2 meals
Pita bread (6-8)

OTHER

Plastic wrap
Aluminum foil
Red wine (3/4 cup) for 2 meals

Custom Eat Sheet™

RECIPE NAME   Page

_____

_____

_____

_____

_____

MEATS

DAIRY

PRODUCE

DRY ESSENTIALS

SPICES

BAKING GOODS

HELPERS

FROZEN FOODS

BAKERY

OTHER

MEATS

Chicken, pre-roasted from the deli (1 whole)
  (2 lbs or 900 g)
  (or use 1 lb or 450 g deli cooked chicken breast)
Chicken breasts, boneless, skinless (4)
  (1 1/2 lbs or 675 g)
Sirloin steak, lean (3 lbs or 1350 g) for 2 meals

DAIRY

Butter
Milk, 1% milk fat (1/2 cup)
Sour cream, no-fat (1/4 cup)
French vanilla yogurt, low-fat (1/4 cup)
Mozzarella cheese, part-skim, shredded (1 1/2 cups)
Parmesan cheese, light, grated (1/2 cup)

PRODUCE

Fresh garlic (from a jar)
Red onion (1/5)
Baby potatoes (20) or 4 large
Baby carrots (1/2 lb or 225 g)
Red bell pepper (1) (optional for Veggies & Dip)
Broccoli florets (3/4 lb or 340 g)
Broccoli and cauliflower (pre-cut and packaged)
  (1/2 lb or 225 g)
Leftover veggies (2-3 cups) (use what's in fridge,
  e.g. onions, celery, peppers)
Toppings for Chicken Burgers (e.g. lettuce, tomato)
Baby spinach (12 oz or 340 g)
Strawberries (6)
Mandarin oranges (1-2)

DRY ESSENTIALS

Lasagna noodles (12) (10 oz or 285 g)
Basmati or white rice (1 1/2 cups)

SPICES

Garlic powder
Garlic & herb seasoning, salt-free
Ginger powder
Lemon pepper seasoning, salt-free
Paprika
Peppercorn seasoning, salt-free
Poppy seeds
Spicy seasoning blend, salt-free
Salt

BAKING GOODS

Cooking spray
Sesame oil
Toasted sesame seeds (optional for Stir-Fry)

HELPERS

Mayonnaise, light
Ketchup
Soy sauce, reduced-sodium
Honey-garlic sauce (1 1/2 cups) for 3 meals
Tahini (1/4 cup) ground sesame paste (can be with
  peanut butter or mid-eastern food or health food)
Tomato pasta sauce, choose a lower sodium brand
  (2 cans, 24 oz or 680 mL each)

FROZEN FOODS

Mixed beans (1 lb or 450 g)
Stir-fry mixed vegetables (1 lb or 450 g)

BAKERY

Whole wheat or multi-grain buns (6-8) for Burgers
Whole wheat or multi-grain buns (4-6)
  (optional for Honey BBQ Roaster Chicken)

OTHER

Zipper lock freezer bag (3 large) for 3 meals
Plastic wrap
Aluminum foil

Conversion Chart

Monitoring Your Fat (for the day)

Percent	If You Eat	Your Daily Fat Intake Should Be
	1500 calories	50 grams
	2000 calories	67 grams
	2500 calories	83 grams
30%	3000 calories	100 grams
	1500 calories	42 grams
	2000 calories	56 grams
	2500 calories	69 grams
25%	3000 calories	83 grams
	1500 calories	33 grams
	2000 calories	44 grams
	2500 calories	56 grams
20%	3000 calories	67 grams

What We Say and What We Mean

Large lasagna or cake pan means approx 9"x13" pan with sides.

Square baking pan means approx 8"x8" or 9"x9" pan with sides.

Cookie sheet means large pan with short edges.

Broiler pan means the pan that comes with your stove. It is large, and has a slotted cooking surface which fits over a bottom pan to catch drippings.

Colander means a large bowl with holes to drain pasta or rinse vegetables in the sink.

Main Component

beef, chicken, seafood, vegetarian
'cause you have an idea of what
you'd like

Prep Code

by color
for when timing is everything

Alphabetical Listing

'cause you remember the name

Fat Content

from lowest to highest
'cause your health requires you to
watch your fat intake

Index by Main Component

Beef

Chicken

Seafood

Vegetarian

Index by Color

Index by Alphabetical Listing

Index by Fat Content

Storing and Use of Ingredients

Sauces & Pastes

Cranberry Sauce -like jam, fabulous addition to savory sauces or reductions, stores great in fridge long term and can be frozen

Honey-Garlic Sauce -add to ketchup or tomato base sauces, use in stir-fries or as a glaze, stores great in fridge long term

Oyster Sauce -fabulous for Asian cooking and stir-fries, stores great in fridge long term

Teriyaki Sauce -fabulous in stir-fry or glaze for meats, stores great in fridge long term

Peanut Sate Sauce and Szechwan Sauce -fantastic for adding to Asian and Indian cuisine, great for dipping and stir-fries

Hot Chili Sauce (sambal oelek) small amount adds heat to a sauce, dressing or glaze, stores great in fridge long term

Tahini (ground sesame seeds) -use as a replacement for peanut butter in recipes for nut allergies (caution some people with nut allergies have seed allergies as well), stores great in fridge long term

Curry Paste - fantastic in Asian and Indian dishes, fabulous mixed with sweet jams for glazes and additions to sauce or reductions, stores great in fridge long term

Salsa -can be added to almost any sauce for flavor and texture, stores great in fridge long term

Dry

Spices you don't normally purchase -can really make the difference in a recipe, store in a dark cupboard, will last a reeeally long time

Salt-Free Spice Blends -easy way to add flavor quickly and sodium free

Onion Flakes -when there's no time to cut an onion, they're great

Brown Gravy Mix, Dry (either chicken, beef or veggie) – thickens gravies and sauces easily, stores great in cupboard long term

Cornflake Crumbs -great flavor, nice substitution for bread crumbs, keep well sealed

Liquids

Vegetable Juice -purchase single serving size if you don't normally use

Orange Juice and Other Juice -purchase single serve portions if you don't normally use

Chicken, Beef and Veggie Broth -canned long term storage, tetra pacs more economical, limited fridge life but are fantastic to add to almost anything, purchase reduced-sodium when possible

Sweeteners
Maple Syrup -add almost anything for a great sauce or glaze, stores great in fridge long term

Honey, Liquid -natural way to sweeten sauces and dressings, stores great in cupboard long term

Jam -fantastic in glazes, sauces and reductions, stores great in fridge long term

Applesauce, Unsweetened -purchase single serve portions if you don't normally use, open only what you need

Fresh
Cheese Tortellini, Fresh -fabulous to boil and serve with brothy soups or to make a pasta sauce for, freezes beautifully

Garlic (from a jar) -I ALWAYS have a small jar on hand for those rushed days

Cans and Jars
Mushrooms, Canned -great to have on hand when you run out of mushrooms

Pineapple, Canned –great to add to salads, pizzas and sauces, both juice and fruit can be frozen

Evaporated Milk -great to have on hand for recipes that require milk...juuust in case you run out

Oils
Nut and Seed Oils, Sesame Oil -often have a high smoke point, great in Mediteranean, Asian and Indian cuisine, sesame often used as a flavoring, stores great in fridge long term

Canola Oil or Vegetable Oil -great for recipes where you want the oil to have a neutral flavor, store in dark cupboard, if not using often purchase in small quantities as it can go rancid

Olive Oil -great for dressings, sautéeing veggies, dipping with vinegar, stores great in cupboard long term, if not using often purchase in smaller quantities

Flavorings
Wine -alcohol burns off when cooking and can assist in cutting down sodium when making a reduction or sauce

Dijon Mustard -great to add to most sauces, stores great in fridge long term

Catalina Dressing -great in sauces or on a salad, can be frozen in same bottle, stores great in fridge long term

Balsamic Vinegar -naturally sweet and tart, fantastic in sauces and glazes, stores long term on pantry shelf

Our Team

Photohouse Studios Inc. - Ian and his crew are simply amazing! It takes a great photographer to agree to shoot food without using photography tricks. What you see is what you get. If that means the meal is ugly...I just think you should know that ahead of time! Don't you? Ian is the owner of Photohouse Studios Inc., St. Albert, Alberta, Canada. www.photohousestudios.com

Gordon Matheson, MD, PhD, is the Chief, Division of Sports Medicine, Stanford School of Medicine, Stanford University and is Editor-in-Chief of The Physician and Sportsmedicine, one of the largest sports medicine journals in the world. I thought it was very cool that he understood the importance of Eating Forward™ and how we need to simplify good information to reach not only the general public, but also the medical areas that don't deal with nutrition for the most part.

Pat Verge - Editor at large! This poor editor had to deal with all my oooooos here and a few !!!!!!!!!!!!!!!!!!! there, but she pretty much managed to keep me in line while letting me ouuuuuuuuuuuuuuuuu and ahhhhhhhhhhh just a little! (You have to understand, for an exclamation junkie, it's really hard to leave this paragraph right now!!!!!) Pat is the owner of Springtide Publishing, Cochrane, Alberta.   patricia.verge@ telusplanet.net

Solange Adams - Supportive Mom Company
My beautiful mother-in-law. Solange worked every day on
the photography set... and showed up with props, flowers and hand picked apples from her tree. What would we ever have done without her?

Tannie Cyr - This is Tannie's last graphic design project with us as she has gone on to bigger and better things! It's been great - our prayers will be with you always!

Illustrations - Lorna Bennett
I don't know how Lorna does it, but drawing after drawing...they're always perfect. Lorna is the owner of Lorna Bennett Illustration, Edmonton, Alberta. www.lornabennett.net

Illustrations - Hermann Brandt
Once again Hermann joins our team. We love to hire local talent, so when we moved we were worried about finding an illustrator we liked as much as Lorna. Hermann had big shoes to fill and he did. Hermann studied art at the Pretoria Technicon Arts School in South Africa. Hermann is the owner of Plein Aire Art Studio, Cochrane, Alberta. www.hermannbrandt.com

Our Team

Ron Richard - Graphic Design and Almost Everything Else
Ron runs the day to day operations of our company and is the lead graphic designer for our books. Sometimes I don't know how he swings it all. I do know I love him and that we are the best team ever! Husband, friend and boss with benefits!
He's also the financial planner, office manager, technical support provider, contract negotiator, food stylist and editor.
Ron Richard is the co-owner (with me) of our own company.
Cooking for the Rushed Inc.   www.cookingfortherushed.com

Graphic Support - Kris Nielson
Kris joins us once again and has taken on a much bigger role. How many people are as blessed as we are to have a pro like this almost at our back door? And he's nice too! Kris is such an easy person to work with. Thanks for making us look so good! Kris is an international award winning graphic artist as well as a published author, photographer and a certified outdoor instructor and guide.
Kris is the owner of Kris Nielson Design, Cochrane. Alberta.   www.krisdesign.ca

Dietitian, Diabetes Consultant - Sandra Burgess B.A.Sc.,R.D.,C.D.E.
Sandra is an enthusiastic member of our team for a third time! She calculated all the Food Exchange and Food Choice values. Her work revolves around making diabetes something people can manage easily. She is an avid volunteer with the Canadian Diabetes Association and Inn from the Cold Society.
Sandra Burgess is a registered dietitian and a certified diabetes educator with 30 years of professional experience.

Kelly and George opened our eyes to the world of doctors. They showed us what they see and how they see it! They opened up their minds to the possibility that most people don't know what the heck doctors are talking about when it comes to health issues. Thanks for being excited about getting out of the box!

George Lambros MD

Kelly Brett MD

189

A Note From Sandi

Half way through the production of this book, it suddenly dawned on us why a book like this has never been written before and why it's so difficult to write! We're in an editorial meeting. The topic--Protein. I ask Kelly and George, "But why should a person care whether they have protein or not? Amino acids, so what??!! Do you really think we are going to change a nation's habits because they are fascinated with amino acids?"

George and Kelly look at each other in disbelief. Won't people care about amino acids? They begin to banter to themselves at the end of the long table. They've now discussed the benefits of protein for about ten minutes. Kelly's eyes are lighting up as the long scientific words flow from his mouth and with every word, I seem more confused. All of a sudden, they realize they're the only ones in the conversation!

It became clear that day how difficult it was to take all this complicated stuff and make sense of it. The docs know my mission is to get into the head of the average person who is bombarded with ever-changing health information. They respect that and I respect them…these guys are really smart!!! When Kelly proclaimed that his favorite word is choledochojejenostomy, we all had a good laugh. (He even knew how to spell it, now that's scary!!!) What happened that day, I pray, will help us, even in a small way, to change the course of how North America sees overall health.

My passion is to get people to be Eating Forward™ so that dinner is off their mind. I want people excited about dinner again. When I heard about these two amazing doctors and their passion to teach people about energy balance in a simplified way - well it was a match made in heaven.

If you read through the pages of this book and say to yourself, "But what you're saying sounds just too easy," this will be music to the ears of Kelly, George, Ron, me and everyone else who put their heart and soul into this project. If you feel the information is easy to read and easy to understand, then we will have accomplished exactly what we set out to do.

Sandi